GARDENING WITH
Perennials

FROM THE EDITORS OF Horticulture

HORTICULTURE
BOOKS
CINCINNATI, OHIO
www.hortmag.com

08 07 06 05 04   5 4 3 2 1

Gardening with perennials / from the editors of Horticulture.
    p.   cm.
   Includes index.
   ISBN 1-55870-721-2
   1. Perennials 2. Landscape gardening I.Horticulture.
SB434.G35 2004
635.9'32--dc22
                              2004043336

Edited by Trish Wesley Umbrell, Thomas Fischer, Teri Dunn and Jennifer Ziegler
Designed by Camillia DeRhodes and Matthew DeRhodes
Art direction by Clare Finney
Production coordinated by Sara Dumford and Mark Griffin
Page layout by Matthew DeRhodes
Photography edited by Tina Schwinder
Indexed by Pat Woodruff

photographic ACKNOWLEDGEMENTS

PHOTOGRAPHY

Tony Avent: p. 20 left, p. 21 left, p. 24

Richard Brown: Cover: top right, p. 118, p. 119, p. 123

Jonathan Buckley: p. 64, p. 66, p. 67, p. 69, p. 114, p. 116 bottom left, p. 130 bottom left

Rob Cardillo: p. 20 right, p. 107 second row: first & fourth photos

David Cavagnaro: p. 35 right, p. 107 third row: first, second & third photos

Michael Davis: p. 107 first row: third photo, fourth row: first photo

R. Todd Davis: p. 17, p. 103 left

John Elsley: p. 30 left

Tom Fischer: p. 61

Roger Foley: p. 23 top

Garden Picture Library: p. 10 bottom left, Christopher Fairweather; p. 25 top right, Howard Rice; p. 33, Mayer Le Scarf; p. 48, Howard Rice; p. 49 left, Howard Rice; p. 95 top left, Juliette Wade; p. 111 right, Sunniva Harte

Galen Gates: p. 15

John Glover: p. 10 bottom right, p. 25 left, p. 41 right, p. 47 top

Pamela J. Harper: p. 103 right

Harpur Garden Library: Cover: top left, p. 6, p. 8, p. 51, p. 53, p. 76, p. 97, p. 109 top, p. 112, p. 113

Lynne Harrison: p. 7, p. 16 top, p. 31 right, p. 34 right, p. 40, p. 42, p. 43, p. 47, p. 63, p. 68 box, top: right & left, center: right & left; p. 81, p. 120 top right, p. 127, p. 131 bottom right, p. 132 bottom: left & right

Andrew Henderson: p. 75 bottom left

Daniel J. Hinkley: p. 83

Saxon Holt: p. 11 top, p. 107 first row: second photo; second row: third photo; third row: fourth photo; fourth row: third photo

Bill Johnson: p. 19, p. 116 center left

Donna Krischan: pp. 84-86

Andrew Lawson: p. 10 top, p. 16 bottom, p. 26, p. 29, p. 30 right, p. 39, p. 41 left, p. 65 right, p. 80, p. 82, p. 95 bottom, p. 96, p. 98 left, p. 129, p. 130 bottom right, p. 131 top left, p. 134 bottom, p. 135, p. 136

Lightworks: p. 59

Charles Mann: p. 71, p. 128, p. 133

David McDonald: p. 68 bottom right

New England Wild Flower Society: p. 120 top left, D. Love; center left, NEWFS: center right, D. S. Long; bottom left, F. Bramley; bottom right: D. S. Long; p. 121, D. S. Long; p. 123 Walt/Louieann Pierowicz

Clive Nichols: p. 49 right, p. 50

Jerry Pavia: p. 20 center, p. 21 right, p. 34 left, p. 35 left, p. 46, p. 130 top right, p. 132 top right

Photonica: p. 105 left, Fred Wright; right, Zeta Fast Forward

Photos Horticultural: Cover: bottom, p. 11 bottom, p. 25 bottom right, p. 27 left, p. 38, p. 45, p. 75 right, p. 94 center, p. 99, p. 100, p. 110 bottom, p. 111 left, p. 132 top left, p. 134 top

Positive Images: p. 101 right, Albert Squillace; p. 102 top, Margaret Hensel

Susan A. Roth: p. 23 bottom, p. 27 right, p. 98 right, p. 116 top, p. 131 top right & bottom left

Lauren Springer: pp. 54-56, p. 58, p. 72, p. 73, p. 77, p. 78, p. 107 fourth row: second photo

Aleksandra Szywala: p. 107 first row: first photo; second row: second photo

Michael S. Thompson: p. 31 left, p. 44, p. 65 left, p. 94 top & bottom, p. 95 top right, p. 101 left, p. 102 bottom, p. 104, p. 108, p. 109 bottom, p. 125, p. 130 top left

Mark Turner: p. 68 bottom left, p. 107 first row: fourth photo, p. 116 center right & bottom right

Christopher Weil: pp. 87-92

White Flower Farm: p. 110, Michael H. Dodge

ILLUSTRATIONS

Raymond Booth/Fine Arts Society, London; from Japonica Magnifica by Don Elick & Raymond Booth: p. 124, p. 126

Jean Emmons: p. 12, p. 13

Elayne Sears: p. 115

TABLE *of* CONTENTS

chapter two
PERENNIALS FOR SPECIAL CONDITIONS

chapter three
DESIGNING WITH PERENNIALS

introduction

Welcome to *Horticulture* magazine's new book on perennials, with a broad range of articles from our recent archives.

While it is always possible to get good basic information on popular perennials in many places — reference books, nursery catalogs, even the tags on the plants down at your local garden center — it takes a magazine like *Horticulture*, a trusted resource since 1904, to deliver the most current and progressive information. *Horticulture* has a niche among all gardening magazines as the one that seeks out the newest, best and most exciting plants.

And our authors are not mere reporters. Dan Hinkley really has traveled to the forests of the Pontic Alps of northeastern Turkey and the moist, shaded forests of eastern Nepal in search of gardenworthy members of the genus *Paris*. The late Graham Stuart Thomas knew the blue poppies of which he writes for his entire gardening lifetime. Lesser-known members of the genus *Aster* populated Tom Fischer's own yard as he acquired and sought to evaluate them.

Sydney Eddison's thoughtful ruminations on how to bring out the best in daylilies in your perennial displays bear the unmistakable stamp of personal experience. These are the keenest of keen gardeners, ones who have not only grown these plants, but also studied up on them. Their assessments are honest and savvy, and their enthusiasm is infectious.

What a thrill it is for us, then, to present to you this anthology, a "greatest hits" of some of our favorite garden writers and the plants they love. In the pages that follow, you'll find cutting-edge information on and inspiring landscaping ideas for a wide range of excellent perennials. But that's not all. You're sure to be struck by the boundless curiosity of these gardeners — a curiosity that, truly, nurtures any gardener's soul. Fresh, expert knowledge is at your fingertips here, but so is many a chance to rejuvenate the look of your garden as you consider the perennials you might grow.

–Teri Dunn

chapter one
PLANT PORTRAITS

AFRICA'S BLUE LILIES

once confined to the conservatory, agapanthus now brightens borders and outdoor containers

by MARTY WINGATE

There are few plant names more exotic than lily of the Nile.

And indeed, these showy, somewhat tender perennials — members of the genus *Agapanthus* — are exotic in every sense of the word, being both strangely beautiful and of foreign origin. Native to a wide area of South Africa that stretches from the Cape Peninsula to the mountains south of the Limpopo River, agapanthus were first cultivated in Europe in the late 17th century. *Agapanthus africanus*, an evergreen species with strappy basal leaves and a globe of lavender-blue flowers atop tall stems, was the first member of the genus to reach foreign shores, where it made a striking, if tender, figure.

Over the centuries *A. africanus* was joined by several other slightly hardier members of the genus. (Even *A. africanus* has now been determined to be hardy to USDA Zone 8, not 9, as was previously thought.) By mixing and matching the characteristics of different species, breeders (and sometimes the plants themselves — agapanthus hybridize freely) have come up with a group of more than 50 hybrids and cultivars for today's gardens.

A Closer Look

Agapanthus divide neatly into two groups: evergreen (four species) and deciduous (six species). Most can be considered hardy perennials in climates with moderate winters — roughly USDA Zones 7/8 to 10. If you garden in an area colder than Zone 7, container culture is your best bet. As a group, the deciduous species — which include *A. campanulatus*, *A. caulescens* and *A. inapertus* — are slightly hardier.

agapanthus IN POTS

The harder something is to grow, the more we want it, and gardeners in areas with far below-freezing winters will willingly haul potted agapanthus in and out of the greenhouse, conservatory or garage to enjoy their late-summer glory. On the positive side, agapanthus make perfect pot plants, growing and blooming well even when crowded. Moreover, potted agapanthus allow you to mix and match with other plants, either in the border or on a terrace or deck. Dwarf selections do fine in a 6" to 8" terra-cotta pot; the big evergreen hybrids, however, may need a container as large as a half whiskey barrel — something to bear in mind when it comes time to move them. As with in-the-ground agapanthus, potted specimens need to be kept well fed and watered during the growing season.

In Zone 6 and colder, store potted agapanthus in an above-freezing garage or greenhouse for the winter. Water sparingly, barely keeping the soil from going dry. In Zones 7 and 8, you can move the pots under the eaves of the house so that the plants will stay slightly warmer and won't become waterlogged.

Although agapanthus look like bulbs — and are even listed as such in many catalogs — they are in fact simply perennials with thick, fleshy roots. The leaves are attached to a single stalk, which some describe as leeklike — an apt term, which helps us see in our mind's eye how the base of each leaf overlaps the next. This short stalk, however, is soon obscured by the leaves, and isn't noticeable unless you go poking around. The plants gradually increase in bulk by sending up offsets around the original stem.

Determining how agapanthus should be classified botanically is a vexed question. For centuries they were considered to be members of the lily family (Liliaceae). More recently, however, they have been placed in the relatively new onion family (Alliaceae). In a recent moment of clarity, there has been a call for the genus to constitute its own family — the Agapanthaceae, a view that prevails among botanists in South Africa.

A Host of Choices

Where agapanthus are easiest to grow, the excitement has dulled. In California, for example, they grow so well they're often used in plantings next to gas stations and fast-food restaurants. Familiarity breeds, if not contempt, then boredom, and some gardeners may cast a jaded eye on a plant so ubiquitous.

But agapanthus can still charm. Their flowering period, from mid- to late summer and sometimes into October, makes them a valuable asset, as does their appealing deep blue to white color range. There is also a choice of tall or short, deciduous or evergreen, dense or open flower heads and solid green or variegated foliage.

When tall, the vertical flower stalks add height to any bed or plant combination, and the flower heads themselves — a ball on a stick — are useful as foils to other plant shapes. When the flower stalks are short, they produce the same effect as the ornamental onion *Allium cristophii* does when combined with bulkier plants. The flower stalks of most species and hybrids have a tendency to lean at a jaunty angle, as if the weight of the flowers was almost too much for them.

Among the shorter selections are the blue-flowered 'Streamline', with lower stalks to only 18", and the 2' 'Tinkerbell', which has white variegated foliage to complement its light blue flowers. The giants include 'Storm Cloud', which blooms in dark blue on a 4' stem, and 'Ellamae', which can reach 5' or more.

As you might expect, many agapanthus cultivars contain the word blue: 'Blue Leap', 'Blue Mist', 'Blue Triumphator', 'Midnight Blue', 'Blue Danube' ('Donau'), 'Kingston Blue', and 'Joyful Blue', to name just a few. All are actually in a range of light to dark lavender blue, although some of the darkest hybrids of *A. inapertus* can be almost navy blue. Several white cultivars exist, too, including 'Bressingham White' and 'White Ice', but the blues far outnumber them.

The flower heads of some selections, such as the dwarf 'Rancho White', are dense with flowers; others are more sparse. In addition to dark color, the deciduous *A. inapertus* has contributed a drooping, starburst form to the inflorescence of its hybrids, along with individual flowers that flare at their tips. The deep violet 'Storm Cloud' and dark blue 'Lydenburg' both exhibit this form. Even more striking are the flowers of *A. inapertus* subsp. *pendulus*, which are more tubular, less campanulate and markedly pendulous. And not just pendulous — the deep blue-violet flowers look as if someone let the air out of their tires. The influence of *A. inapertus* can also be more subtle. The slightly pendulous, halfway tubular flowers of 'Bressingham Blue' are the only clue to its heritage.

Many cultivars involve *A. campanulatus*, a deciduous species. These include the well-known Headbourne hybrids, a strain that bears bell-shaped flowers in shades of light to medium lavender. Plants with flowers that are fused at the base and open up to form a widely flaring star are likely to include *A. campanulatus* subsp.

Agapanthus 'Midnight Blue'

facts and
FIGURES

TYPE OF PLANT: herbaceous perennial **FAMILY:** Agapanthaceae (agapanthus family) **ORIGIN:** South Africa **HEIGHT:** 18" to 5', depending on cultivar **LEAVES:** narrow and lance-shaped to broad and strap-shaped; gray green to medium green, depending on species or cultivar **FLOWERS:** borne in a many-flowered umbel; bell-shaped and upright to tubular and pendulous; dark blue-violet through white **BLOOM PERIOD:** midsummer–October **HARDINESS:** USDA Zones 8–10 **EXPOSURE:** full sun in most areas; partial shade in areas with hot summers **SOIL:** rich, well-drained **WATER NEEDS:** moderately heavy while in active growth **FEEDING:** feed annually in spring with a balanced fertilizer **PROPAGATION:** by division in spring **PROBLEMS:** none

Agapanthus 'Liliput'

Agapanthus inapertus 'Lyndenberg'

Agapanthus inapertus subsp. hollandii

Agapanthus 'Bressingham White'

Companions for Agapanthus

When you're deciding what to plant with agapanthus, keep in mind that older leaves of many cultivars lie flat on the ground. That precludes any really close neighbors, but does make for good weed suppression.

Agapanthus begin the summer as a foliar presence, and then, starting in July or August and lasting into October, add their flowers to the display. It's tempting to combine agapanthus with true lilies (Oriental or Asian) to echo the flower form, but to create contrast with the vertical agapanthus, something with a more horizontal line is called for. *Heuchera* 'Amber Waves', with shockingly colored foliage of apricot and gold, is a perfect candidate. Another exciting pairing is with late-flowering clematis, such as the red-violet 'Etoile Violette', trained over a chicken-wire frame. The darker blue agapanthus selections, such as the brooding *A. inapertus* hybrids, make a fine contrast to the cheerier yellows of late summer, such as *Helenium* 'Butterpat' or *Crocosmia* 'Norwich Canary'.

Your climate will dictate whether agapanthus are year-round garden denizens or temporary summer stars, but even the splendor of a few short months is worth it for the distinctive addition these stellar plants will make to your garden.

growing TIPS

Grow agapanthus in well-drained soil rich in organic matter and fertilize as growth begins in spring. Keep the plants evenly watered during the growing season. In regions with intense summer heat, grow agapanthus in part sun. Full sun is best in cool summer climates (such as in the maritime Northwest, where we consider an 80°F day to be sweltering).

In USDA Zones 8 to 10, agapanthus can be left in the ground. However, in Zone 8 and even warm parts of Zone 7, a thick mulch of straw is a good idea. (Some catalogs list agapanthus as hardy even to Zone 6, but that's getting chancy.)

Evergreen selections need to be divided every three to four years to keep them floriferous. Deciduous cultivars, in contrast, are best left undisturbed as long as possible — even in pots they grow best when crowded. Division should be done in spring by removing the smaller offsets from the parent plant and repotting them or replanting them elsewhere.

patens in their lineage. In the selection 'Baby Blue', this effect is accentuated by a darker lavender midrib running down each petal.

Although the wild form of the evergreen *A. africanus* is difficult to grow, it is represented by much easier cultivars for today's garden, including the well-known dwarf 'Peter Pan', with medium blue flowers on 18" stems, and 'Ellamae', at 4' to 5' with purple nodding flowers. But things get tricky here; evergreen or semievergreen selections may owe that trait to either *A. africanus* or *A. praecox*, another evergreen species.

ARUMS, ETCETERA

hardy members of this largely tropical family bring a strange beauty to temperate landscapes

by RICHARD W. HARTLAGE

Although most of the 104 genera and 3,200 species of the arum family (Araceae) are tropical — the scarlet anthuriums common in florists' shops are an example — there are several temperate genera with outstanding ornamental value, especially for gardeners with an eye for the unusual.

Arisarum proboscideum

With their distinctive heart-shaped leaves and sometimes bizarre flowers, these plants, known collectively as aroids, seldom go unnoticed.

The best-known hardy aroid is probably jack-in-the-pulpit, *Arisaema triphyllum*, native throughout woodlands from southern Canada to Louisiana and as far west as Kansas. Much more exciting to the horticulturally adventurous are those arisaemas from China, Japan, Taiwan, Nepal and India. One of the most captivating is the Japanese *A. sikokianum* (hardy in USDA Zones 5–9; to 16"). The exterior throat of the spathe is purple brown; the elliptic hood, which comes to an elegant point, is the same color as the base but distinctly striped in greenish white. Most striking of all is the pure white spadix, which resembles a mortar and nestles in the white interior of the spathe. Some forms also sport silver flares in the center of the five-segmented leaves, adding to the plant's appeal. A word of warning: *A. sikokianum* tends to emerge from the ground very early in the spring and can be damaged by frost. If it is killed to the ground, it will not grow again until the following season, so be sure to plant it in a protected location.

In contrast, *A. candidissimum* (Zones 5–9; to 20"), from western China, is a dawdler; in fact, in northern areas, it may not emerge until July. This subtly beautiful plant bears waxy, ivory flowers suffused with pink that nestle among glossy, apple-green, tripartite leaves. There are two forms in circulation: one fragrant and one not. (Most aroid flowers, if they have a fragrance at all, are putrid-smelling.) True, you have to get on your hands and knees to experience the lemony scent, but when present, it is delightful.

One of the most sought-after arisaemas is the Himalayan *A. griffithii* (Zones 7–9; 16"), which belongs to a group of species commonly known as cobra lilies. Large tripartite leaves loom over the flowers, which are held near to the ground. The flower is mahogany brown suffused with plum, and wider than it is tall. Two auricles — earlike structures — protrude on either side of the spathe to give the effect of an alarmed cobra. Heightening the effect is a long stringlike appendage, which can reach 3' on older plants, that grows from the tip of the hood. The overall impression is memorably sinister.

All arisaemas like bright filtered light and humus-rich soils with even moisture. For the plants to perform their best, a top-dressing of compost or well-rotted manure should be applied in late winter or early spring.

Arisaema sikokianum

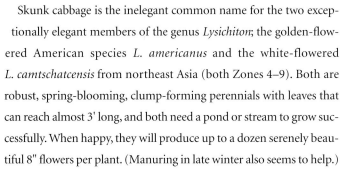

Skunk cabbage is the inelegant common name for the two exceptionally elegant members of the genus *Lysichiton*; the golden-flowered American species *L. americanus* and the white-flowered *L. camtschatcensis* from northeast Asia (both Zones 4–9). Both are robust, spring-blooming, clump-forming perennials with leaves that can reach almost 3' long, and both need a pond or stream to grow successfully. When happy, they will produce up to a dozen serenely beautiful 8" flowers per plant. (Manuring in late winter also seems to help.)

Mature plants resent being moved or divided, so be sure to start with young specimens. They are also easy to grow from seed, and when the two species are grown in proximity they will hybridize, producing sterile offspring with creamy yellow spathes. If you want to engage in a bit of home hybridizing, simply pour water through the spathe of the male parent and catch it in a cup, then pour this slurry of pollen over the spadix of the female parent and wait for the seed to ripen. Don't forget to mark the crosses by tying a colored string around the hybridized flower stems. (This method can be used to hybridize arisaemas and arums as well.)

At the opposite end of the scale, in terms of size, is the mouse plant, *Arisarum proboscideum* (Zones 6–9; 6"), a rhizomatous aroid that is quick to establish in shade or part sun. Brush aside the elongated, heart-shaped,

Arum italicum subsp. *italicum* 'Marmoratum'

growing aroids FROM SEED

Growing hardy aroids from seed is an easy way to obtain rare species. Before sowing, soak the seeds in warm water overnight to rehydrate them and to remove any pulp. Sow the seed in 4" pots in a well-drained seed starting mix. Because the seedlings should not be transplanted for at least two years, it's best to sow no more than fifteen seeds per pot. Cover the seeds with about .25" of grit; this will encourage germination and inhibit liverworts and mosses. Label the pots with plant name, date and source. In USDA Zones 8 and warmer place the pots in a protected spot outdoors so that the seeds will be exposed to cold temperatures, which are necessary for germination with many species. (Most arisaemas germinate quickly and do not require a chilling period.) In colder areas, place pots in a cold frame for the winter. Once the seedlings have germinated, place them where they get bright, diffused light and fertilize them with liquid fertilizer at half strength. Pot the seedlings individually at the start of their third growing season. Don't overwater the pots when the seedlings are dormant, for they rot easily at this stage.

8" leaves to catch a glimpse of the curious brown-and-white flowers, borne in late spring, whose spathes taper into a 6"-long "tail." Not an exceptionally showy plant, but one that appeals to the child in all of us.

Gorgeous-leaved Species

Among the 26 species of the genus *Arum* — which has lent its name to the entire family — are several that are highly gardenworthy. All native to the Mediterranean basin and Europe, they tend to grow actively from fall through spring and go dormant in summer — an adaptive trait to hot, dry summers and mild, rainy winters. One of the best known and most useful is the plant widely known as *A. italicum* 'Pictum' but correctly as *A. italicum* subsp. *italicum* 'Marmoratum' (Zones 6–10; to 18"). Grown primarily for its beautiful silver-veined foliage, which emerges in October

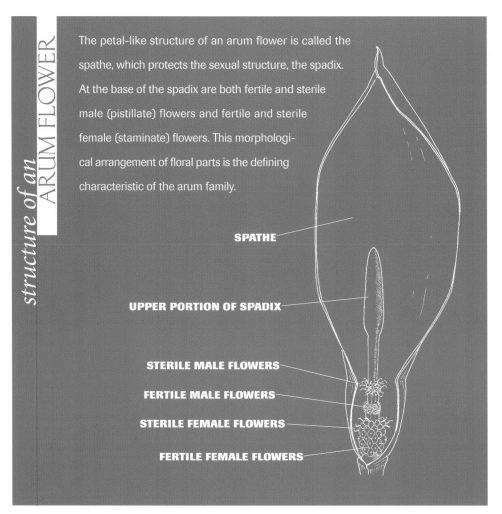

structure of an ARUM FLOWER

The petal-like structure of an arum flower is called the spathe, which protects the sexual structure, the spadix. At the base of the spadix are both fertile and sterile male (pistillate) flowers and fertile and sterile female (staminate) flowers. This morphological arrangement of floral parts is the defining characteristic of the arum family.

SPATHE

UPPER PORTION OF SPADIX

STERILE MALE FLOWERS

FERTILE MALE FLOWERS

STERILE FEMALE FLOWERS

FERTILE FEMALE FLOWERS

and goes dormant in late April, this arum is also notable for the club-like mass of scarlet fruits that develop in August or September from the inconspicuous, fleeting, translucent green flowers. If you're lucky, you may come across selections such as 'White Winter' in which as much as 70 percent of the leaf surface is silver. (Plants grown from seed of these choice cultivars come reasonably true; they can, of course, also be divided.) *Arum italicum* will grow in either sun or shade, and tolerates drought but not excessive moisture. It will often self-sow.

The showiest arum in flower is *A. creticum* (Zones 7–9; 18"), whose creamy yellow spathes, produced in late April to early May, are nothing less than sumptuous. They are also sweetly fragrant. Give this species plenty of sun and sharp drainage to ensure that it will flower well.

With their grassy foliage and spathe-less flowers, the marsh-dwelling members of the genus *Acorus* are most unaroid-like aroids. The sweet flag, *A. calamus*, got its common name from its aromatic rhizome, which, dried and powdered, is used in the perfume industry as a fragrance fixative. Of greater interest to gar-

deners, however, is the white-variegated form, *A. calamus* 'Variegatus' (Zones 4–9; 2' to 4'), which makes a striking vertical accent, especially when contrasted with round-leaved plants that also relish wet soil, such as ligularias or darmeras. The lower-growing *A. gramineus* (Zones 5–9; 6" to 16") has several intriguing variants. One of my favorites is the extremely dwarf (to 3") golden-leaved *A. g.* 'Minimus Aureus'. Because it will withstand light foot traffic, I like to use it in small tufts between stepping stones. Another outstanding form is golden-variegated 'Ogon', introduced from Japan by Asian plant expert and nurseryman Barry Yinger. Growing to 1' or so, it spreads slowly to form large mats. If you examine the plant closely, you will discover that each leaf is striped in chartreuse on canary yellow.

The next time you see a vase of anthuriums in a flower shop window, let it be a reminder of all the strange and wonderful possibilities the aroids have to offer. Granted, some are very odd indeed, but others are strikingly beautiful and will add depth and interest to any garden.

THE OTHER ASTERS
some of the lesser-known species offer a galaxy of promise

by THOMAS FISCHER

For as long as I have been gardening I have had an affection for the fall-blooming hybrid asters — the offspring, for the most part, of *A. dumosus*, *A. novae-angliae* and *A. novi-belgii*.

Who could fail to be seduced by their billows of color, so clear and soft in the autumn sunlight? But in recent years their shortcomings have begun to weigh more heavily: nondescript foliage; intolerance of drought, shade and poor soils, and a susceptibility to ills (especially among cultivars of *A. novi-belgii*). Thus, with a fond backward glance, I have turned my attention to other members of the genus, figuring that there are bound to be neglected treasures among so large a group (the genus numbers some 250 species). And so there are. Of course, there are also quite a few weedy horrors, but once we get past the thugs and uglies, there are plenty of species that offer not only beauty of flower and foliage, but also amenability to a wide range of growing conditions. And most of those I have experimented with don't need staking. (I have noted the few exceptions.)

Amateur botanists will no doubt be quick to realize that the plants described below are all natives of North America, mostly to the northeastern and midwestern United States and Canada. This is purely accidental; the European and Asian species that might have qualified simply struck me as being inferior, either in ornamental qualities or in ruggedness of constitution, to the plants I have chosen to include.

Tall Species for Sun

At the top of my list of favorites is the smooth aster, *A. laevis* (hardy to USDA Zone 4; 3'–5'). In fact, I like it so much that I grow four different cultivars of it in my small sunny border, where every square foot is precious. My original plant, the plain species, came from Montrose; Nancy Goodwin's nursery of happy memory in Hillsborough, North Carolina. It forms a modest clump, to 4', clothed in attractive, dark green, oblong leaves that are 5" long at the base of the plant. But it is the stems that first catch your eye: they are a dark violet, almost black. When the abundant, clear lavender-blue, yellow-eyed flowers do open in September, the effect is utterly seductive. Even more beautiful is the English cultivar 'Calliope', which was selected in the early years of this century at the Royal Horticultural Society's garden, then at Chiswick. It, too, has black, wiry stems, but the young foliage is tinged with

Aster lateriflorus 'Lady in Black'

violet and the plant is more robust, reaching 5' or 6', and the flowers, which hold off until October in my garden, are nearly 2" across. Of markedly different character are an American selection, 'Blue Bird', and the extremely vigorous German selection 'Blauschleier' ("blue veil"). Both form dense clumps to 4', clad in narrow, somewhat glaucous leaves. In September, the top third of the plant erupts into a multitudinous haze of small, lavender-blue flowers. Although both cultivars are lavish, even prodigal, in bloom, they unfortunately lack the dramatically dark stems of other forms of the species. All forms of *A. laevis* will put up with dryish soil — a trait that should endear them to resource-thrifty gardeners — and have been free of maladies in my garden.

A plant of similar effect is *A. turbinellus* (Zone 4; 4'), a species that the crusty and opinionated Reginald Farrer praised for its "grace and astonishing delicacy of beauty." It is an erect plant to 4' or 5', with reddish stems clad in narrow, pointed, slightly drooping leaves that can be as long as 8" near the base, but become feather-fine at the top — the effect is like a shaving brush. The blue-lavender flowers appear in September. Although they are only about 1.5" across, they are well displayed at the ends of the stems and so look larger. This seemly plant has grown well for me in a spot that gets only morning sun. Although it blooms as much as I could wish, I do need to stake it, a chore that I suspect I could dispense with if I moved the plant to a sunnier location.

Aster lateriflorus 'Prince'

Aster ericoides

Near *A. turbinellus* I have planted a most unasterlike aster, *A. umbellatus* (Zone 3). It has a formal carriage and the clean, light green, phloxlike leaves are perpendicular to the stems. It gets 5' tall in my very ordinary soil, and references say it can reach 6'. What sets this species apart are the curious, flat-topped umbels of small, creamy white flowers — almost like those of an achillea — that appear from late September into October. Gertrude Jekyll included this aster in the gray-and-purple end of her long border, and certainly it makes a splendid foil for purple- and lavender-flowered asters, as well as for late-blooming monkshoods and delphiniums

in their second flowering. One warning: This aster loathes drought. Weekly soakings are needed during dry spells to keep the foliage from going limp.

The most regal of the tall, sun-loving asters I grow is something of a puzzle. I raised it from seed obtained from an arboretum in the Midwest; the packet was labeled "*Aster drummondii*" (Zone 3), and that is what I have called the plant, although its appearance doesn't jibe with the references I have consulted. Printed accounts describe the species as growing from 2' to 5' and having bright purplish blue flowers in dense clusters. My plant is a strapping 6', and in early September becomes a mass of small, skim-milk-blue flowers so dense that you can scarcely see a leaf. Given the extreme variability of so many *Aster* species, I am willing to believe my plant is the genuine article, but whatever its true identity, I treasure it for its superabundant flowering and refreshingly icy color — like the palest clones of *Campanula lactiflora*.

Midsize Sun Lovers

It may be just wishful thinking, but it seems to me that the medium-size aster species — those that grow from 1' to 3' — have been gaining in popularity in recent years. They certainly deserve to be widely grown, for they are easy to accommodate in a garden of modest proportions and many have foliage that is an asset even when the plants are not in flower.

A plant outstanding for the quality of both leaf and blossom, and one much underused, is *Aster lateriflorus* (Zone 3; 1'–4'), sometimes known as the calico aster. It is most commonly encountered in the form of its cultivar 'Horizontalis' (2'–3'), a plant remarkable for the way in which the stiff, twiggy branches grow at right angles to the main stems. These are clothed with tiny leaves that assume a purple tinge in late fall, which is also when the numerous, .5" flowers open. The flowers are a pale lilac with a rosy center, and make the whole plant into a richly harmonious blend of pale and dusky shades. The plant's almost shrubby appearance inspired Christopher Lloyd to use it as a hedge at his garden at Great Dixter — an idea too good not to be appropriated and tried over here. (To paraphrase T. S. Eliot's remark about poets and their sources of inspiration: Immature gardeners imitate; mature gardeners steal.) An old but sturdy hybrid of *A. laterifolius*, 'Coombe Fishacre', deserves mention; it is similar in habit and coloration to 'Horizontalis' but a bit taller at 3' to 4'.

Aster lateriflorus 'Prince' (2') bears foliage as fine as that of 'Horizontalis', but its stance is upright. Even though its habit is more conventional, it wins the prize for foliar color, for the leaves emerge a dark purple in the spring and stay that way all season long. In June, it can accompany scarlet Oriental poppies; in July, the brilliant panicles of *Crocosmia* 'Lucifer', and finally in autumn it can shift gears and meld with the blues, whites and lavenders of its fellow asters. A newer selection, *A. l.* 'Lady in Black', caused much excitement among European nurserymen — it has the dark foliage of 'Prince' but reaches an impressive 6' in height. Not exactly midsize, but at the back of the border its tower of somber violet leafage would be quite a sight.

Fine, almost needlelike foliage also characterizes the aptly named heath aster, *A. ericoides* (Zone 3; 1'–3'). This charmer appeared unbidden in a messy part of my yard near the woodpile and nearly got yanked out. Fortunately, I kept putting this task off until the fall, at which point I would as soon have composted a clematis as pull up the aster, now covered with dainty sprays of .5" white flowers with yellow eyes. (There's a moral in there somewhere.) Although the white-flowered forms are my favorites — 'Cinderella' at 3' and 'White Heather' at 2' are particularly nice — the pastel tints of 'Blue Star', 'Pink Cloud' and the rosy lavender 'Ringdove' (all about 3') are also lovely. There are a few taller-growing selections — the creamy white 'Brimstone' and mauve 'Hon. Vicary Gibbs', 4' and 5', respectively — but they usually need staking. Like *A. laevis*, *A. ericoides* will put up with a fair amount of dryness.

Two other midsize species I have regretfully had to put into the "if at first you don't succeed" category. *Aster grandiflorus* spent all summer and most of the fall growing into a dense, somewhat floppy, 2.5' plant with small, narrow leaves. In late October, it erupted into 2" flowers of a glorious royal violet that shone like beacons clear across the garden. Not a trace of it appeared in the spring, and perhaps as a native of the Southeast it is not hardy in coastal New England. But I'm not ready to give up yet. *Aster sericeus* was another heartbreaker. I grew this species from seed, cosseting and fussing over the wan and refractory seedlings. Only one survived, and in time it grew into a 2' plant covered with small, oval, silvery gray leaves (*sericeus* means silky), unlike anything I had seen in an aster. In August, blue-violet flowers 1.5" wide appeared to complete the picture. Here, I thought triumphantly, is a gem for the gray garden. Then it died. (There's a moral there, too.) I'll be ordering seed again.

Asters for the Shade

There are times when I almost lose patience with the white wood aster, *A. divaricatus* (Zone 3; 1'–2.5') — a denizen of our garden, I suspect, long before we bought the place — and its tendency to seed itself about, but when I take a good look at the plant, with its handsome, heart-shaped leaves and elegant brown-black stems, I relent. Besides, how many other ornamentals will thrive in the dense, dry, rooty shade underneath our big red oak without the least attention? I wish the white flowers, which appear from late summer into the fall, made more of a show — they're just under 1" across and rather gappy. I recently acquired the selection 'Roger Raiche', which is reputed to have larger flowers than the ordinary species; I hope it does, and that it has an improving effect on the local gene pool.

With a certain amount of trepidation I have just given garden space to another shade-loving quasi-thug, *A. macrophyllus* (Zone 3; 2'–2.5'). A number of books describe the foliage of this species as coarse, and I suppose it is, if you consider bergenias and *Brunnera macrophylla* coarse. I think it is splendid, and ample reason to grow the plant. These bold, handsome leaves are cordate, or heart-shaped, and the lowermost ones can be as long as 8". The flowers, alas, are a great disappointment: although they are sometimes borne in considerable quantity, they sport only 9 to 18 ray florets apiece and are a washy mauve. For these reasons I prefer the white form, 'Albus', whose flowers at least don't disappear in the sylvan gloom

Aster drummondii (lavender) with *A. pilosa* (white)

and might optimistically be described as starry. But let's get back to those aggressive tendencies. It is not by self-sowing that *A. macrophyllus* launches its campaigns of imperial conquest, but by rhizomatous romping, and I may live to regret turning it loose in the garden, having fought many a pitched battle with the likes of *Lysimachia clethroides* and *Macleaya microcarpa*. But if it will clothe our dry shady bank in decent greenery and crowd out the hawkweed, it can romp to its heart's content. At least for a while.

Much better behaved and infinitely more appealing in flower is *A. cordifolius* (Zone 3; 1'–6'), which goes by the pleasant name of blue wood aster. Although it won't thrive in the miserable conditions that *A. macrophyllus* puts up with, it is happy in the high, dappled shade of deciduous trees and in humusy soil that doesn't get too dry. Like *A. macrophyllus*, *A. cordifolius* has rough, heart-shaped leaves, although they are smaller, reaching only about 5". Most of the commonly available selections of this species are on the tall side, up to 6', and may need staking, depending on the density of the shade in which they are grown. From late summer into midautumn *A. cordifolius* bears dense clouds of small (.5"–.75") flowers, usually in some variant of blue or lilac. The disks, which are pale yellow at first, soon turn a rosy purple. It is cheering to know that a couple of lovely older selections of this species are still available, namely the 6'-tall, palest blue 'Aldebaran' and the 3', pinkish lavender 'Elegans'. The superb cultivar 'Little Carlow', a 3'-tall plant with vivid lavender-blue flowers, is often listed as a selection of *A. cordifolius* but is in all probability a hybrid — its flowers are noticeably larger and it seems to want full sun.

Last summer I was greatly pleased with the performance of a species new to me, *A. anomalus* (at least Zone 6; 2'–3'). Planted in a fairly dark, dank spot, it grew bolt upright to about 2', clad in attractive, elliptical, light green foliage, and in August put on a respectable show of 1.5" pale blue flowers. Most attractive and, to my mind, not at all anomalous. This past spring, however, I realized I should have deadheaded it before it went to seed: one entire bed threatened to become an *anomalus* nursery.

At the very least, by planting some of these species we can help our gardens escape the dreariness that results from a limited and predictable plant palette; at best, we can turn them into dynamic laboratories for our passions and enthusiasms. Indeed, as much as I admire and enjoy all of the plants I have described, I can't help wondering what might result if an imaginative nurseryman were to use them in a breeding program — perhaps an aster with crimson flowers and bold purple foliage, or a shade lover with large pink flowers and black stems. The possibilities seem endless, and endlessly tantalizing.

REVENGE OF THE REDNECK LUPINES

when it's hot, dry and daunting, baptisias beat the pants off their temperamental cousins

by TONY AVENT

Please forgive me, but I'm in my baptisia phase. Fellow plant lovers will understand and sympathize with my compulsive need to study and collect every form of baptisia in sight before moving on to something else.

This particular phase started many years ago, but it wasn't until after several unsuccessful attempts at growing baptisia's sister genus, the lupines, that I went off the deep end for this group of glorified peas. No matter which varieties I tried, lupines failed outright. Worse, they produced plants of such ugliness that mercy killing seemed the only appropriate action. All the while, only a few feet away, my baptisias — which I've renamed "redneck lupines" — thrived.

There are some 23 species and subspecies of *Baptisia* in the United States, found from the East Coast to the Midwest. Their common name, false indigo, was coined by early Americans who substituted baptisia for true indigo (*Indigofera* spp.) in the production of blue dye. Though they may be unappreciated old hound dogs, baptisias have a lot to offer gardeners — an attractive ruggedness, outstanding dependability and great structure for several weeks in the spring garden, from the early-flowering *B. leucophaea* to the late-flowering *B. australis* var. *minor*.

Baptisias are amazingly tolerant of drought and impervious to the ravages of nature — a point driven home on one of my early baptisia-collecting trips to northern Texas during the first week of August, when local weather reports were lamenting the area's fiftieth consecutive day over 100°F and its sixth month without rain. I was truly amazed to find wild baptisias looking as good as they would have in

Baptisia 'Screamin' Yellow'

a well-watered garden, with full seed capsules intact. Who said agaves and yuccas could be the only structural elements in a xeriscape garden?

Winter hardiness, too, is one of the great surprises about baptisias. They all seem to be winter hardy through USDA Zone 5, and possibly Zone 4. Both Brian McGowan of Blue Meadow Farm in Massachusetts and Hans Hansen of Shady Oaks Nursery in Minnesota have performed trials on many of the southern species with amazing success.

Baptisia species flower in many shades of blue, from near purple to light blue, as well as white, creamy yellow and bright yellow. Between natural hybrids and intentional crosses, though, it won't be long before we see reds and pinks joining the mix.

The Blues

Although blue is the best-known baptisia color, blue varieties are actually the least common. *Baptisia australis*, the most commonly grown blue species, is a gardenworthy plant, but hardly a star of the genus. Native to riverbanks from Vermont south to Pennsylvania's Shenandoah Valley, *B. australis* is one of the larger species, forming mounds of blue-green foliage 3' tall by 5' to 6' feet wide. The large, 24" flower spikes emerge atop the new foliage in mid-April in North Carolina. By late April, the flowers begin to open in shades ranging from sky blue to vivid dark purple. (Most species tend to bloom several weeks later in the North.) Over time, as the weight of the forming seed increases, the flower spikes on *B. australis* become lax and wobbly.

I think the best of the blue-flowered species is *B. australis* var. *minor*. It's virtually unknown commercially because a few taxonomists made the decision that it was no different from *B. australis*. Having studied it in the wild, however, I'm convinced that it's significantly different from *B. australis*. For one thing, it makes a much smaller plant that rarely exceeds 18" tall. Its leaves are also much smaller, and have a much lacier texture. The real beauty of *B. australis* var. *minor*, however, is that its 12" to 18" spikes of blue or lavender flowers don't get lazy and flop over like the spikes of *B. australis*. Additionally, it produces huge, 1.5", thumblike seedpods that turn a magnificent pure black when they mature.

Cool Whites

The white baptisia species have suffered from muddled nomenclature for so long that most gardeners have no clue about which ones they're growing. The most commonly seen names in books and catalogs are *B. alba*, *B. leucantha* and *B. pendula*. However, when the smoke from the taxonomists' guns finally cleared, *B. alba* had been switched to *B. albescens*; *B. leucantha* changed to *B. alba* var. *macrophylla* and *B. pendula* dropped for *B. alba* var. *alba*. Thank goodness we have taxonomists to straighten out the messes made by their predecessors.

With a few exceptions, the white-flowered species are much later flowering than most of the blue- or yellow-flowered species. *Baptisia alba* var. *macrophylla*, which is found from Minnesota

Baptisia sphaerocarpa   *Baptisia alba* var. *alba*   *Baptisia sphaerocarpa* (close up)

south to Tennessee, is one of the tallest species, ranging from 5' to 7' tall, and although individual clumps don't produce many flower spikes during its May/June blooming period, each regal flower is a thing of beauty.

Baptisia alba var. *alba*, or thick-pod wild indigo, is the southeastern form of *B. alba*, and can be found scattered throughout the Southeast, from North Carolina to Florida. It is easily distinguished from *B. alba* var. *macrophylla* by its large, black, pendent seedpods and shorter (3'–4') stature.

Another southeastern native, *B. albescens* ranges from Tennessee to Florida. It is prized as a garden plant for its smaller stature, which is usually 4' or less, and its numerous, charcoal-black, long-racemed flower stalks. Unlike other white-flowered species, the seedpods of *B. albescens* turn tan as they dry rather than black. I found a specimen of *B. albescens* on a dry, central–North Carolina road bank that was 7' tall; just imagine what it will do for you in good garden conditions.

Yellows: Subtle to Shocking

One of my favorite baptisias is the little-known *B. bracteata*, which can be divided into *B. b.* var. *bracteata* (native from North Carolina south to Alabama) and *B. b.* var. *leucophaea* (synonymous with *B. leucophaea*, and found from Texas north to Minnesota). All the varieties of *B. bracteata* flower very early, often starting in late March to early April here in North Carolina. Unlike other baptisias, the flower stalks of *B. bracteata* emerge horizontally, like giant clusters of creamy yellow grapes. Moreover, many regional forms of *B. bracteata* var. *leucophaea* emerge with a dark purple cast to their new foliage, which disappears as they come into flower.

Most people agree that the best of the yellow species is *B. sphaerocarpa* (also known as *B. viridis*). It's hard to find any other baptisia with as much flower power as this native, which can be found from Texas to Missouri. Not only is it particularly showy, but it tolerates all sorts of conditions. I have found this species growing in the wild in dry sand as well as in wet swales. In the wild, a stand of *B. sphaerocarpa* looks like a glowing mass of lit candles. This only gives a hint of what the plant can do when given some tender loving care in the garden. Here at our nursery, we have grown single specimens that attained a height of 2' with a spread of 4', and produced over 130 flower spikes at one time. Additionally, *B. sphaerocarpa* produces perfectly round, marble-size seedpods, which are quite distinct from species with more finger-shaped pods.

While none of the other yellow species flower as showily as *B. sphaerocarpa*, there are some that stand out for their foliage. *Baptisia perfoliata*, for one, has wonderful, glaucous, eucalyptus-like foliage. Endemic to a couple of southern highways (particularly Interstate 20 in South Carolina and Georgia), *B. perfoliata* plants can eventually reach 30" tall and 3' wide. Though it produces yellow flowers in its leaf axils in April, *B. perfoliata* achieves its

Baptisia minor

Baptisia australis

facts and FIGURES

TYPE OF PLANT: herbaceous perennial **FAMILY:** Papilionaceae (pea family) **LEAVES:** single or trifoliate **HEIGHT:** 1'–7', depending on species **FLOWERS:** blue purple, white or yellow **HARDINESS:** USDA Zones 4–9 (most species) **EXPOSURE:** full sun **SOIL:** clay to sand, preferably dry **PLANTING TIME:** anytime the ground is not frozen **WATER REQUIREMENTS:** very drought tolerant once established **PROBLEMS:** few; not eaten by livestock

BAPTISIAS AT A GLANCE

SPECIES	BLOOM TIME IN NORTH CAROLINA	HEIGHT	FLOWER COLOR	NOTES
B. alba var. alba	May–June	3'–4'	white	great vertical accent
B. a. var. macrophylla	May–June	5'–7'	white	great vertical accent
B. albescens	May	4'	white	charcoal-black flower stalks
B. australis	May	3'	blue-purple	very wide and robust
B. australis var. minor	May	1.5'	blue-purple	airy texture, nice black seedpods
B. bracteata	March–April	1'–1.5'	creamy yellow	goes dormant early
B. cinerea	April	less than 1'	bright yellow	horizontal flower panicles
B. perfoliata	April	2'–3'	yellow	cool, eucalyptus-like foliage; goes dormant early
B. sphaerocarpa	April–May	2'–3'	bright yellow	floriferous; round seedpods
B. 'Carolina Moonlight'	May	3'	light yellow	very vigorous
B. 'Purple Smoke'	May	4'	purple	slow to establish but worth the wait
B. 'Screamin' Yellow'	April–May	2'–3'	yellow	full, neat habit

PROPAGATION

Most baptisias in the United States are propagated from seed. But since they are promiscuous (at least with other baptisias) and seed blocks are rarely isolated, expect variance from seed-sown plants. Fresh-sown baptisia seed germinates quite easily — usually in about two weeks — when planted in a light potting mix that doesn't hold excess water. Barely cover the seeds, and keep them indoors between 50°F and 90°F. If the seeds are sown outside in the fall they will germinate the following spring. Old stored seed, on the other hand, can be very difficult to start and slow to sprout. To break down the seed coat and encourage germination of old seeds, I recommend soaking them in a foam cup of boiling water and leaving them there until the water has cooled.

Most baptisias will root easily from stem cuttings in spring, when their growth is soft, though the success rate plummets to zero once the plants harden. Dip the cuttings in a rooting hormone and keep them in high humidity until they root, which usually takes about eight weeks.

Overwintering newly rooted baptisia cuttings can be problematic, however, if the plants haven't had time to store enough starches before winter. We've found that plants placed directly into the ground after they have rooted will develop starches and buds faster than those kept in containers. A second option is to keep newly rooted, containerized plants in a warm greenhouse or on a windowsill until their buds develop, and then place them outside to go dormant.

It has been unquestioningly accepted for years that baptisias don't like to be moved or divided. As with many old gardener's tales, however, this one has no basis in fact. I have successfully divided and transplanted baptisias in winter, in summer and in flower during the spring. I've even had bare-root divisions survive that were stored in plastic bags for over a week. Obviously, the person who started this rumor wasn't a good gardener.

...ustralis (seed pods)

I like to use baptisias as specimen plants and place them where their structural form can be appreciated. Planting them among groundcovers highlights their best attributes. One of my favorite companion plants is *Artemisia* 'Powis Castle', whose silver foliage echoes the blue in the baptisia foliage. I try to plant the artemisia several feet away from the baptisia, so that only the outer branches surround its base.

I also like to pair baptisias with veronicas, including 'Sunshine', 'Aztec Gold' or 'Georgia Blue', since I particularly like to play yellow against blue. Other groundcovers that serve as perfect foils for baptisias include *Iris tectorum*, which usually coincides with mid-spring baptisias, like *B. bracteata* var. *leucophaea*, and any of the gold-foliaged acorus, provided the ground doesn't get too dry in summer. Baptisias are also perfect plants to follow early-spring-flowering bulbs.

coolest look in late summer, after its leaves have browned and its small, round seedpods have dried. It makes for a unique garden addition, with tremendous floral arrangement possibilities.

For smaller spaces, *Baptisia cinerea* — a native of the North Carolina/South Carolina sandhills and coastal plain — is a great but often overlooked choice. Resembling *B. bracteata* var. *leucophaea* but rarely exceeding 1' in height, *B. cinerea* is adorned with horizontal flower panicles of bright yellow in early spring, usually April. For a cheery dose of yellow in the spring perennial border, this is a great choice.

Selections and Hybrids

Considering the worldwide proliferation of cultivars, there are perplexingly few named selections of *Baptisia* in the trade. One that has not yet hit the market in a large scale is native plant guru and nurseryman Larry Lowman's *Baptisia sphaerocarpa* 'Screamin' Yellow', which, at 2' to 3' is slightly shorter than the other forms we grow.

The North Carolina Botanical Garden in Chapel Hill has an extensive baptisia collection, so it's not surprising that new cultivars have arisen from the horticultural hanky-panky going on there. Rob Gardner, the curator at NCBG, has made two introductions from the collection so far. Gardner's amazing first introduction, *B.* 'Purple Smoke', was a cross between *B. australis* var. *minor* and *B. albescens*. 'Purple Smoke' picked up the 4'-tall, black flower stalk from *B. albescens* and the bluish purple flower color from *B. australis* var. *minor*. Thanks to the latter parent, 'Purple Smoke' also flowers in late May, though we've found that it takes about three years to produce a spectacular specimen with full-size blooms.

The second of the NCBG releases is 'Carolina Moonlight'. A cross between *B. sphaerocarpa* and *B. albescens*, this amazingly vigorous and fast-growing plant reaches a height of 3' and has upright spikes of light buttery yellow in late April to early May. 'Carolina Moonlight' is the first baptisia with creamy yellow

Baptisia bracteata var. *leucophaea*

flowers held on anything other than pendulous spikes. Well-grown plants of either of these hybrids will hold their own against any lupine, and will far outlast them.

We are currently working with a number of keen gardeners and researchers from around the country who are breeding and selecting baptisias for size, stem color, flower color and even a more diverse flowering season. It will only be a matter of time before nurseries will be offering dramatically improved selections. Who knows? In a few years, maybe you and I will meet at the first Redneck Lupine Society meeting.

BLUE NOTES

by ANN LOVEJOY

As a very young gardener, I loved borage for its willing ways. Every one
of its barrel-shaped seeds seemed to sprout as soon as it was planted.

Cerinthe major 'Purpurascens'

Mertensia virginica

Myosotis scorpioides

Fuzzy stems and foliage gave the lanky plants a substantial look and the summer-sky-blue flowers sparkled in a quiet sea of green and gray herbs. As I grew older and got to know the plant better, however, its very willingness made it less desirable. Those dazzling blue flowers still made a delightful framework for Madonna lilies, and the cucumbery-tasting leaves and buds did indeed lend piquancy to salads. But borage's eager incursions into every bed in the garden turned my early enthusiasm to guarded acceptance.

Nonetheless, any plant so determined to prosper has its place, particularly when it provides sought-after shades of blue. These days, I grow annual borage (*Borago officinalis*; 2'–4') in rough places — along the back driveway, near the compost bin — where its wild ways are an advantage. In its former place, I grow a small host of more mannerly borage kin, which provide a brilliant blaze of blue flowers over a long season without taking over the garden. The borage family (Boraginaceae) as a whole is distinguished by an ease of cultivation that often borders on excess. The most gardenworthy members, however, earn their way in the most refined gardens.

By far the most asked-about plant in my garden last summer was purple honeywort (*Cerinthe major* 'Purpurascens', 1'–3'), an annual borage relative with handsome foliage and exotic, colorful bracts that long outlast its small flowers. Like its kitchen cousin, purple honeywort's flowers are tubular bells of intense blue or purple, delicately scalloped and lined in cream. The bells are clustered in twos and threes, each group nesting inside brilliantly blue bracts overlapping like fish scales. The true leaves are rounded, lustrously gray blue in color, and as fleshy in texture as a succulent. The new growth is stippled with creamy stripes and flecks that fade to a subtle marbling as the leaves mature. This variable species has several forms with yellow or purple-red flowers, all of which make handsome companions for flaming crocosmias such as sizzling orange 'Firebird' and fire-red 'Lucifer'.

Those who find common forget-me-nots (*Myosotis sylvatica*; USDA Zone 3; to 18") too ratty (or too rampant) can choose among some 50 species for more sophisticated forms. In boggy or damp sites, water forget-me-nots (*M. scorpioides*; Zone 3; to 2") will

Symphytum ×uplandicum 'Variegatum'

Myosotidium hortensia

Pulmonaria 'Spilled Milk'

provide a long-lasting array of charming blue, pink or white flowers. Gardeners in very mild climates can attempt the elusive Chatham Island forget-me-not, *Myosotidium hortensia* (Zone 8/9; 2'–3'), a beauty with broad, glossy leaves and the annoying habit of vanishing just when you think it has settled down for you. In shady gardens, elegant Siberian bugloss (sometimes called heartleaf forget-me-not; *Brunnera macrophylla*; Zone 3; to 2') makes a stylish companion for crested ferns and blue seersucker hostas. For hotter, sunnier spots, try biennial Chinese forget-me-nots (*Cynoglossum amabile*; to 2') instead, mingling them with a flurry of silk grass (*Stipa tenuissima*) and another biennial borage, purple bugloss (*Echium vulgare*; to 18").

A number of popular borage cousins are indispensable in woodland gardens. Round-leaved, tender blue Virginia bluebells (*Mertensia virginica*; Zone 3; to 2') can be interplanted with columbines and hostas to create a lasting tapestry of foliage and flowers. A Japanese beauty, *M. maritima* var. *asiatica*, offers blue-lustered, spoon-shaped leaves and pale blue flowers. Hailing from sandy island beaches, it demands totally different conditions from its Virginia cousin, requiring perfect drainage and full sun.

Spotted, speckled, streaked and striped, the lungworts (*Pulmonaria* spp.) have such fascinating foliage that their uncoiling flower heads (usually combining shades of pink, rose, blue and purple) are often overlooked. Pulmonarias have proliferated in recent years, leading to an explosion of new forms, many crossed between various of the 14 species. Several hybrids (all hardy to Zone 5) have pewtered foliage and pinky blue flowers, such as 'Spilled Milk' (to 1') and 'British Sterling' (1'). 'Roy Davidson' (18") has long, slim and heavily speckled leaves and sumptuous blue flowers. The almost entirely creamy, green-edged foliage and coral flowers of *P. rubra* 'David Ward' (to 18") set it apart from the crowd. All the lungworts hold their beauty longest when given fertile, evenly moist soils and dappled shade.

Navelworts (*Omphalodes* spp.) offer flowers of the appealing blue invariably identified as "innocent," as well as a Quakerly white. Only a few of the 28 species are widely grown, but spring beauty, *O. verna* (Zone 5; 3"–6" by 3'), was a beloved garden plant in

Europe even before Marie Antoinette popularized the use of its charming blossoms in tussie-mussies. Middle eastern *O. cappadocica* (Zone 6; 6"–10") has several well-selected forms, notably 'Cherry Ingram', a prolific producer of large blue flowers. Fetching 'Starry Eyes' makes an airy patch of twinkling, lavender-edged blue blossoms in mid-spring. Softer 'Lilac Mist' has the same delicate flower color but without the snapping blue eye. Though their bloom is fleeting, the navelworts are enduring woodlanders that gently lace their way through larger plants.

If your garden is sunny and has acid soil, you may prefer the lithodoras, compact crawlers and creepers that are often evergreen where winters are mild. *Lithodora diffusa* 'Grace Ward' (Zone 5; to 1') is perhaps the best known of the bunch, though creeping 'Heavenly Blue' (3"–5") runs a close second. When pleased, both offer masses of vividly blue flowers over a protracted period. In hot climates, afternoon shade will improve their performance. In seaside or mild-summer areas, however, these plants excel in full sun. A fast-spreading relative, *Buglossoides purpurocaerulea* (Zone 4; to 2'), thrives in dry, gravelly soils, but it produces its silvery blue flowers best when given a bit of shade.

Naturally, every good family has a few skeletons in the closet. The comfreys are nearly as encroaching as plain borage, and many a gardener has come to curse their persistent roots. Variegated forms, however, are generally better behaved. The best of these are workhorses for shady spots, notably dapper *Symphytum ×uplandicum* 'Variegatum' (Zone 4; 3'–4'), whose cream-striped pyramids of foliage stand out with distinction against a backdrop of glossy rhododendrons. Comfreys such as *S.* 'Hidcote Pink' are durable

groundcovers, running with vigor even under cedars. The ivory-splashed *S. ibericum* 'Variegatum' and yellow-tinged 'Goldsmith', on the other hand, need moist shade and less root competition.

Where it finds conditions to its liking, *Trachystemon orientalis* (Zone 4; to 2') acts like a comfrey, roaming widely and producing vast quantities of big, hairy leaves. The blue flowers are pretty, yet far too flopsy and fleeting to balance the mass of greenery. I am frankly baffled by its high horticultural status.

My own favorite borage is heliotrope (*Heliotropium arborescens*; Zone 10; to 6'). Generally treated as a deliciously scented annual, this tropical shrub can be wintered over in a warm greenhouse, where it continues to flower while winter winds howl. This plant has the best manners of all the borages: Not only do its midnight-purple flowers smell like warm cherry pie with vanilla ice cream, but never once has it proved itself profligate in any of my gardens.

THE SOARING CIMICIFUGAS

versatile bugbanes offer a combination of elegance and durability

by C. COLSTON BURRELL

Plant names tell stories that capture the imaginations of gardeners. The images conjured up by the name bugbane, however, are not necessarily pleasant.

But the stately cimicifugas (the generic name derives from the Latin *cimex*, meaning bug, and *fugo*, meaning to flee or repel) are no bane to gardeners. Quite the contrary — they are a boon: that rare combination of elegance, adaptability and durability, traits they share with other members of the buttercup family (Ranunculaceae) such as clematis, delphiniums, hepaticas and columbines. (A word of warning: gardeners should know that there has been a somewhat controversial name change. Recent taxonomic work by James Compton at the University of Reading, England, has transferred all bugbanes to the genus *Actaea*. Thus far, the nursery industry has not wholeheartedly embraced this change, so keep looking for these plants under *Cimicifuga* for now.)

One of the cimicifugas' most romantic names is wandflower. True, individual flowers of the wand have little to recommend them — they are but a cluster of straplike petals and stiff stamens. When collected together, however, they make a spectacular show. The flowers are followed by dry pods called follicles that contain flattened brown seeds. The seeds loosen in the splitting follicles and vibrate in the wind, giving rise to yet another common name; rattletop.

The foliage of all bugbanes rivals the flowers in beauty. The large, compound leaves are ternately divided — that is, they branch into three equal segments — and they may be subsequently divided up to three additional times, lending them a delicate, feathery look. Plants grow from stout rootstocks with eyes like diminutive peonies. Mature clumps form multiple, tightly packed crowns with congested foliage and a dozen or more wands of

Cimicifuga racemosa

flowers. Cimicifugas are found in North America and in Eurasia. Like many plants with this dual distribution, the species diversity is richest in the southern Appalachians and in temperate Asia.

The American Species

North America is home to six species of bugbanes. The best known is black cohosh, or cohosh bugbane (*Cimicifuga racemosa*; USDA Zones 3–9). A shallow creek wound lazily through the woods at the base of the slope where I first encountered black cohosh in the wild. Under a shadowy canopy of beech and oak, the tall spikes of fuzzy, ill-scented flowers towered over a delightful assortment of yellow lady's slippers, rue anemone, bellworts and ferns. At 5' to 8' tall, this plant is not for the faint of heart. Mature clumps sport multiple stalks that branch high on the scape like a pitchfork. The wands of white flowers open in mid-May or early June in southern regions, and into July in the North. The leaflets of the thrice-divided foliage are deeply cut into ragged lobes. Its native range is from Massachusetts to Missouri and south to Georgia and Tennessee, though it has been widely planted in other areas.

Although American bugbane (*C. americana*; Zones 4–8) is smaller than black cohosh, they are nearly identical in foliage. Thankfully, two differences exist that make it simple to tell them apart. First, American bugbane blooms much later, in August and September. And second, each flower has two or more pistils, so multiple, long-stalked pods are found on each branch of the wand. A quick inspection of the dried stalks will set the record straight. Plants are native to rich woods in the mountains from Pennsylvania to Georgia.

The loveliest and least-known native species is Kearney's bugbane (*C. rubifolia*; Zones 4–8). It has long been sold as *C. racemosa* var. *cordifolia*, a name with no botanical standing. Plants are also commonly mislabeled in nurseries. If you get the real plant, you will know it right away: the leaves are twice ternately divided, with broad, shiny leaflets. The huge terminal leaflet is three-lobed, heart-shaped and coarsely toothed. In all, there are only three to nine leaflets, compared with up to 36 in the other species. Plantsman Graham Stuart Thomas aptly likens them to the leaves of Japanese anemone. The foliage forms a broad parasol only 2' above the ground, although in bloom the plant can reach up to 4'. The slender, branched spikes are gathered in a stiff, upright bunch at the center of the clump. In nature it is restricted to limestone coves in the mountains of Virginia, Tennessee and Kentucky.

Two additional cultivated species, *C. laciniata* and *C. elata*, are native to Oregon and Washington. Though eminently gardenworthy, they have yet to gain wide distribution. Tall bugbane (*C. elata*; Zones 4–8) grows 3' to 6' tall. The twice- to thrice-divided leaves have lobed, heart-shaped leaflets; flowers are borne in summer on leafy, sparsely branched stalks. Cut-leaf bugbane (*C. laciniata*; Zone 4–8) has a squat, many-branched, leafy bloom stalk to 5' tall. The leaves have deeply incised, serrate leaflets, lending a delicate appearance to the open mounds of foliage. The plants bloom in summer.

The Eurasian Species

Two species, *C. dahurica* and *C. foetida*, are found as far north as the colder regions of Russia — good news for northern gardeners who may find them easier to grow than bugbanes from the southern United States. Dahurican bugbane (*C. dahurica*; Zone 3–8) is a

Cimicifuga simplex 'Hillside Black Beauty'

Cimicifuga matsumurae 'White Pearl'

charming plant, with tight foliage mounds and tall, mid- to late-summer inflorescences that stick out from the main stem at every angle, giving the plant a startled look. Plants are dioecious; male plants have more lax inflorescences. The flowers are sweet-scented. The foliage is two to three times divided, with toothed, ovate leaflets. The native range of this plant stretches from Siberia to Mongolia, China, Korea and Japan. Fetid bugbane

Cimicifuga simplex 'Brunette'   *Cimicifuga heracleifolia*

(*C. foetida*; Zones 3–8) has deeply lobed, serrate leaflets. This plant is seldom seen in America, though keen gardeners in Europe enjoy the sparsely branched, arching spikes of creamy flowers on 3' to 6' stems in late summer. Plants are native from Siberia to East Asia.

The hotbed of lustworthy bugbanes is temperate Asia, home of the popular autumn-flowering bugbanes, *C. simplex* and *C. ramosa*. They are very similar in all respects, though historically they have been considered separate species. (The current literature places *C. ramosa* within the species *C. simplex*.) Autumn bugbane (*C. matsumurae*; Zones 4–8) has two popular cultivars. 'White Pearl' has soft green leaves and pale green buds that open to fragrant, snow-white flowers in September and October. Plants are variable in height, as this selection is probably seed-grown. 'Elstead', which I first saw in Beth Chatto's extraordinary garden in England, grows to 3' tall and has striking purple-black stems. The purple-tinted buds open to pure white flowers. This choice plant is just now becoming available in this country.

The real lookers of the group are the purple-leaved forms of *C. simplex* (listed in the trade under *C. ramosa*). Several cultivars are on the market, and each new introduction is an improvement over its predecessor. 'Atropurpurea' emerges a luscious, rich purple black in spring, but as the leaves expand and temperatures rise, it fades to light purple green, darkest along the edges of the leaves. The German selection 'Brunette' commands a hefty price at the nursery, but by midsummer is only slightly darker than 'Atropurpurea'. The color of both selections is highly dependent on temperature — hot nights slowly drain the purple coloration from the leaves. Unfortunately, from Virginia south, plants tend to fade to green and shed their lower leaves in the evening swelter. 'Hillside Black Beauty', selected at Hillside Gardens in Connecticut by Fred and Mary Ann McGourty, is the most colorfast selection to date. In trials by Wayside Gardens' in South Carolina, plants retained their

rich purple-brown color throughout the season. The flowers of all selections have a heady perfume that fills the garden in autumn when it is most appreciated.

The Sly Stallone of the genus is Komarov's bugbane (*C. heracleifolia*; Zones 3–8). Plants produce thick, arching, 6' stems from open clumps. The flower spikes, which bloom in late summer and autumn, bend like shepherds' crooks. The six to nine three-lobed leaflets are thick and coarsely toothed. The leaves cluster at the base of the plant, making the lofty flower stalks all the more dramatic. This tough and attractive plant is found from Russia to China. The variety *bifida* has bold, twice-divided leaves.

These giants have some diminutive but dashing relations. Those with small gardens will appreciate the varieties of Japanese bugbane (*C. japonica*; Zones 4–8). These lovely autumn-flowering plants have ground-hugging foliage and slender, leafless, erect stalks of evenly spaced, starry white flowers. Unlike other species, the flowers are scentless. The taxonomic conundrum afflicts this group as well. Plants sold under the name *C. japonica* var. *acerina* (sometimes listed as *C. acerina*) have twice-divided leaves with up to nine palmately lobed leaflets. The stiff, sparsely branched, hairy bloom stalk rises to 3'. According to cimicifuga expert James Compton, this plant is actually a clone of *C. biternata* (Zones 3–8). More robust, with striking foliage, is the true *C. japonica*. The leaves have only three huge, broad, glossy, toothed leaflets. The showy, dense spikes of white flowers are carried well above the foliage in mid- to late autumn. Established clumps are quite dramatic.

Using Bugbanes in the Garden

Bugbanes are sensational garden plants of easy culture. As woodland wildings, they prosper in a humus-rich soil that retains moisture throughout the growing season. They seem indifferent to soil pH as long as there is ample organic matter to buffer the soil. Plants tolerate a wide range of light conditions, although all species appreciate afternoon shade and in warmer zones require sun protection if they are to perform well. They are best sited in a partially shaded spot, with some direct light. They bloom well even in deep shade, but the flower wands may lean toward the light.

Few plants are easier to place than the bugbanes, since spikes are always needed for accent, especially in the shady garden. I grow most of the species and selections, and each has its appropriate spot. I use the tall, dense spikes of black cohosh like a gauze screen in a bed that separates my terrace from the neighbors' house. The erect stems accommodate low plants underneath the clump of leaves. About its feet a carpet of foamflower is punctuated with astrantias, wild bleeding heart, columbine and sedges. Nearby *Ligularia dentata* 'Desdemona' contributes the requisite bold foliage to contrast with the finely textured cohosh. Next to the June-blooming cohosh is one of the purple-leaved forms. Its September flowers extend the bloom season, and the dark foliage complements the rich red leaves of the ligularia. By placing this fragrant beauty near the terrace I can easily revel in the scent. In spring, when the foliage is at its richest hue, the sultry goblets of 'Queen of the Night' tulips make a suitably solemn display, enlivened by a carpet of the soft yellow *Aquilegia canadensis* 'Corbett'.

I have also seen purple-leaved bugbanes brilliantly used at Chanticleer, a public garden near Philadelphia. The wall of the shaded terrace is lined with a thick golden row of variegated hakone grass punctuated at even intervals by soaring clumps of bugbane. The effect is mouth-watering.

PROPAGATION

One cimicifuga seed capsule produces a dozen seeds, and a handful will keep you in bugbanes for decades to come. The fall-blooming species seldom have time to ripen seed in my garden, though others set a good crop. Raising plants from seed does require patience, however. Once seed has been sown, the pots should be kept at 40°F for three months; during this period, the first root, or radicle, develops. The pots should then be moved to an area with temperatures of about 70°F so that the shoot can develop.

Clumps of bugbane mature quickly and can be divided after only a few years. Lift plants in late summer or autumn after they have finished flowering. Clear enough dirt away from the rootstock so you can see the individual crowns. Then use a sharp knife or shears to separate a portion of the rootstock with a cluster of eyes. If production is your goal, cut the entire rootstock into sections, each containing an eye. Plants can also be lifted in early spring, as the shoots are just breaking ground. They look similar to peonies at this stage.

In my rear garden, a clump of 'White Pearl' bridges the gap between the canopy trees and the epimediums, trilliums and gingers below. The scent in autumn fills the air. I have placed a large patch of *C. biternata* in front of a drift of male ferns, whose fronds provide a restful complement to the coarse bugbane leaves in spring and summer, and a lush backdrop for the September flowers. Kearney's bugbane, one of my favorites, forms a focal point at the end of a narrow path. The early-fall spikes jut up from an underplanting of epimediums and sweet woodruff. For a specimen, there is no better choice than *C. japonica*, with its huge, coarse leaves. My four-year-old plant, still an infant, will eventually fill a corner of the garden against a hedge of viburnums.

Despite their nomenclatural confusion, the bugbanes are an enchanting group of plants. I would be hard pressed to choose the best of the genus. Luckily, many species are available, so I do not have to. I can grow them all, and I do.

A WEALTH OF DIANTHUS

garden pinks are as treasured today as they were centuries ago

by Alfred R. Hermes

Dianthus caryophyllus

Carnations and pinks had already been longtime favorites in gardens when, in 1737, Linnaeus gathered them into a new genus and named it *Dianthus*. The name he chose was a reflection of the great esteem in which the flowers were held, for it means "divine flower," and cultivated forms, far removed from their wild forebears, were already numerous.

Dianthus serve many purposes — in rock gardens and walls, in the border where low-growing plants are desired, in beds massed for grand color displays or simply looking out from sunny corners. Many are suitable for window box and container growing and they are, of course, cut flowers par excellence, whether as lordly carnations adorning rites of passage or as modest bouquets of cottage pinks on the kitchen table.

The genus is a large one, of about 300 species, and its range is immense, comprising temperate and subarctic Eurasia with a few representatives in Africa and Alaska. Generally speaking, *Dianthus* species can be described as annual, biennial or perennial herbs with opposite leaves, often gray or bluish and narrow to the point of being grasslike. The five-petaled flowers may be borne on loosely branching stems or in clusters, and the margins are usually serrated. The predominant color is pink or pale magenta, but white is common, reds deepening to purple appear and yellow is present, though rare. Markings of one or more colors are frequent, sometimes as rings or zones, intricate radial patterns or merely irregular fleckings.

In nature, dianthus are variable and some show a propensity to hybridize. In cultivation, both variability and the opportunity for hybridization increase, so given the abundance of species and centuries of domestication, it is not surprising that the number of named cultivars, most of them extinct, is past counting. Today's dianthus — and there are more than 250 kinds available in the United States alone — are still somewhat daunting in their profusion. But even a nodding acquaintance with some of these and their cultivars may help not only to thread partway through the maze of names and forms, but also to enhance the pleasure of growing these lovely and versatile flowers.

Border Carnations

In America, we tend to think of carnations as florists' flowers, but border carnations have long been grown in Europe, and cultivars more suitable for our continental climate are available to American gardeners. (The dianthus considered here are all hardy, some into USDA Zone 3, and are fairly easy to grow.) *Dianthus caryophyllus*, a short-lived perennial native from western Europe to India, is considered to be its principal ancestor. A clean-limbed plant to 3' tall with narrow gray-blue leaves, its 1.5" to 2" flowers are most commonly pink, but white and many gradations of red also occur. The flowers have a spicy, refreshing fragrance — a property much valued in old, unsanitary, pestilence-ridden times — and it may have been this as much as the visual appeal of the flowers that won the carnation an early following. The zeal of these late-Renaissance devotees of the carnation recalls the late-17th-century tulip craze in Holland. Fanciers of the flower formed associations, held shows, awarded prizes, and choice specimens changed hands at hefty prices.

Along the way, *D. caryophyllus* acquired characteristics unknown in the species: yellow flower color, which appeared around 1600 and suggests an early dalliance with the yellow *D. knappii* of the Balkans, and a "perpetual-flowering" habit. The latter, appearing in France in the 18th century, was an important

Dianthus 'Doris'   *Dianthus deltoïdes* with *Geranium* 'Johnson's Blue'

breakthrough and paved the way for those modern greenhouse carnations that attain the perfection of still-life paintings and are available year-round. These pampered beauties behave well only under the protective glass and the strict regimen of careful growers, but their comely, more modestly proportioned kin, the border carnations, have all the colors, doublings and patterns of the greenhouse types, albeit on a reduced scale.

Older varieties had a discouraging floppiness, and without support could be ruined by even a light shower. Sturdier, more compact cultivars, such as 'Dwarf Fragrance' and the Knight series, need minimal staking and better endure the rain, wind, wide swings in temperature and other rigors of life outdoors.

Cottage Pinks

The carnation appears to have been, in its early stages, the coddled plant of the affluent. The cottage pink (*D. plumarius*) was equally old in cultivation — perhaps older — but tended to be grown in gardens of an unpretentious kind. Also known as the grass, snow or Scotch pink, it is native from Central Europe to the Caucasus. Easy from seed, it is a very hardy, mat-forming perennial that needs little attention other than to be kept free of weeds. In June, from its low cushion of narrow, grayish leaves, an abundance of 1" flowers, fragrant and often deeply fringed, arise on 10" to 15" stems, giving the blooms a fluffy, feathery appearance. Pink is the most common color, but the full dianthus range also appears. It was much treasured by humble folk whose lives often left scant margin for growing flowers. Perhaps typical were the Huguenot refugees who settled in Paisley, Scotland, to practice their trade as weavers and are remembered in garden annals for growing the cottage pinks in great variety.

Modern versions of *D. plumarius* such as 'Spring Beauty' and the slightly earlier-flowering 'Sonata', bear huge quantities of double, pleasingly scented flowers in all the dianthus colors and can occupy a place of honor in the very finest of June gardens, serving equally well in the front of the border, rockeries, stone walls or containers. And, if sheared back after the first explosion of color in June, they have the very welcome habit of producing a few blooms through the rest of the season, sometimes until frost.

Cheddar Pinks

Dianthus plumarius is thought to be the principal ancestor of the modern cottage pinks, but several other species native to the western part of the dianthus range were also cultivated at an early date. *Dianthus gratianopolitanus* takes its awkward name from an ancient city in southern France where Grenoble now stands. It is widespread in Europe and was once particularly abundant in the dramatic rock formations in Cheddar in southwestern England. To English-speaking gardeners it became the Cheddar pink, giving that pleasant town, already known for Cheddar gorge and its tasty cheese, yet another claim to fame. Like the cottage pinks, the Cheddars are mat-forming perennials, but much more compact, with narrow, grayish leaves and fragrant, sharply toothed, bright pink flowers. Garden forms are numerous. 'Petite', 'Rose Dawn' and 'Red Dark Eye' reflect in their names the characteristics that distinguish them from the type. 'Dottie', a gem for the rock garden, has tuftlike foliage and deep red and white flowers. A more recent and outstanding cultivar assigned to the Cheddar group is 'Bath's Pink', found in an old Georgia garden. It bears astonishing masses of sweetly scented pink flowers with a darker eye.

Dianthus chinensis

Dianthus plumarius 'Spring Beauty'

Rainbow Pinks

A species that has been particularly conspicuous over the past two centuries is a migrant from the Far East, *D. chinensis*, sometimes called the rainbow pink. Liberty Hyde Bailey, the dean of American horticulture in his time and a confirmed dianthophile, was not impressed by the wild *D. chinensis* he found growing on rocky hillsides in China — scraggly, unbecoming plants with small, single, lilac-rose flowers lacking fragrance. But the *D. chinensis* that had reached Europe in the early 1700s, probably by way of the Ottoman Empire, were far advanced from their weedy forebears. About 1860, a brilliant new strain of Japanese origin, the Heddewigii pinks, was introduced, and *D. chinensis* and its derivatives have held a secure place in the affections of gardeners ever since. Their range of forms and colors is astounding. There are pure whites through the deepest reds, and the designs of color upon color are endlessly varied. Some will be almost perfect disks, some will have widely separated petals, and others are doubled or frilly. Although perennial, they come so quickly from seed that they are frequently grown as annuals. Named varieties are plentiful, and standard spring fare in garden centers are such popular cultivars as 'Baby Doll', 'Snowfire', and 'Princess' — all thrifty, low-growing plants that come in a fine assortment of colors and forms.

Maiden Pinks and Sweet Williams

Standing somewhat apart from the commonality of the garden pinks are two old-fashioned favorites, the maiden pinks (*D. deltoides*) and the sweet William (*D. barbatus*). The maiden pink is said to take its common name from its habit of partially closing its petals at dusk. This seeming shyness, however, is deceptive, for *D. deltoides* is one of the most aggressive of the entire dianthus clan. Mat-forming, it defends its territory very efficiently, unlike some of its cousins, whose looser growth is easily invaded by weeds. In my garden it is the only dianthus that self-sows with abandon and occasionally makes a minor nuisance of itself. But this is a small price to pay for the company of the maiden pink. In early June, a crowded multitude of 10" to 12" stems,

Most dianthus are short-lived perennials, but they seem to do their best in their second year and are so easily raised from seed that I have found it more satisfying to treat them as biennials rather than to nurse them into decrepit old age. Choice specimens can be propagated by division or by cuttings rooted in a suitable medium. Some cultivars have been kept going in commerce for more than a century this way. All dianthus prefer a well-drained, neutral to slightly alkaline soil and, in regions where acid soils prevail, generous applications of ground limestone will produce noticeable benefits. Full sun is commonly recommended, but the sun of our hot American summers is not like that of alpine meadows or tempered maritime climates where most of the dianthus have evolved. Here, they will be grateful for some midday shade.

Long-cultivated plants usually have a long list of enemies, and dianthus, unfortunately, are no exception. Many of the recorded pests and diseases, however, are likely to appear only in large-scale plantings, and the problems encountered by the home gardener will probably be such familiar evils as damping-off of seedlings, cutworms, slugs, aphids, red spider mites and sowbugs with which the gardener is eternally at war anyway. Probably as effective as anything else is holding the enemy at bay with a thorough fall cleanup and clean cultivation throughout the growing season. Every pest has to come from somewhere, and every weed and piece of debris should be regarded as a potential refuge for the foe.

each bearing several .5" flowers, arises from a 3" cushion of small, green leaves. In the cultivars, hues of a brilliance and intensity appear that might be garish in larger flowers, but, divided as they are among hundreds, make one of the most delightful features of the early summer garden. Varietal names such as 'Flashing Light' 'Leuchtfunk' and 'Brilliant' are well chosen for cultivars that bear these concentrated colors.

The sturdy sweet Williams, native to mountainous regions from the Pyrenees to the Balkans, have been cultivated for more than 400 years. They bear their small flowers in richly crowded clusters, which come in all of the dianthus colors and in sizes ranging from the ground-hugging 'Midget' to the 2' 'Hollandia Hybrids'. Crossed with *D. caryophyllus*, they produced the sterile and temperamental "mule pinks" so much admired by Victorian gardeners.

The Allwoodii Hybrids

Carnations and pinks were once distinct groups in the minds of gardeners. Carnations were *D. caryophyllus*, wonderfully changed through the centuries of cultivation and selection. Pinks were of mixed provenance, but dominated by *D. plumarius*. There had been hints of casual liaisons between the two, but it was not until 1910 that something like formal nuptials were proclaimed when a British nurseryman, Montagu Allwood, advertised his "New Perpetual-flowering Pinks," hybrids of *D. caryophyllus* and *D. plumarius. Dianthus ×allwoodii*, as the new plants became known, had been nine years in the making. Allwood's objectives were plants that were easy to grow, of attractive habit, having a wide color range, strong-stemmed and with a long season of bloom.

The claimed parentage of Allwood's hybrids was not universally accepted. William Robinson, then a most influential figure in British gardening, wrote that *D. ×allwoodii* was a false name and that there was no such plant, and sent letters of protest to the London *Times* and the Royal Horticultural Society. Robinson's unmannerly remarks — he actually used the word fraud — were based on the ground that he had grown thousands of pinks and carnations and had never once seen "a trace of a hybrid" between them. The gardening public, however, took the new pinks to heart. To this day several of Allwood's hybrids are widely grown: the vermilion 'Robin'; the deep pink 'Helen' and 'Doris', an extremely fragrant, semidouble salmon pink. In a world where plant varieties often come and go quickly, this staying power is evidence of genuine merit.

Lest gardeners think that all possible permutations of dianthus have been exhausted, it now appears that an additional role for them is in the making, that of flowering houseplants. Work at Colorado State University has as its goal fragrant dwarf carnations that will flower for several weeks in the difficult environment of the average home. Word is that many rare species are being used in this program, so it may be that in the not-too-distant future, some new faces will appear in the family of dianthus, Linnaeus's divine flower.

PEONY ROOTS

The species offer a simple beauty often missing in modern hybrids

by DANIEL J. HINKLEY

For well over a century, hybrid peonies have been a mainstay
of American gardens along our northern-tier states.

From Maine to Nebraska to Alaska, May brings a flurry of double,
blowsy heads from a host of garden classics such as 'Festiva Maxima',
'Lorna Doone', 'Sarah Bernhardt', and 'Lord Kitchener' — enticing
names that often reveal their Victorian and Edwardian origins. At the
same time, however, these names obscure the plants' ancient genetic
heritage, and their overstated splendor belies the simpler charms of
their forebears. In sharp contrast to their highly bred offspring, wild
peonies offer both a pure, raw beauty as well as a brawny disposition
that easily competes with, and in many cases triumphs over, those al-
loyed by hybridization. According to taxonomists, there exist only 40-
odd peony species in both the Old and New World, with most occurring
in southern Eurasia. They occupy a wide variety of habitats, from shaded, moist, mountainous slopes in China to parched and rocky lowland
pastures in Greece. In fact, their greatest strength, from the gardener's
point of view, may well be their ease of transition from the wilds to the
garden, all the while providing an elegant presence in flower, fruit and
foliage. (Unless otherwise noted, the species discussed here may be
considered hardy to USDA Zone 4.)

Herbaceous Species

Perhaps the most celebrated species is *Paeonia lactiflora*, which the
Welsh gardener A. T. Johnson called "a plant adorned with the grace
of a thousand years of adoration by the Chinese before it entered our
shores." Aberrant forms were treasured by the Chinese emperors, while
in later years the species itself made an enormous impact on contemporary peony-breeding programs. Ranging throughout the rigorous
climes of Tibet into Siberia, it is one of the hardiest of all species. In
mid-spring, large, satin-textured, fragrant white flowers centered by a
boss of golden stamens appear from knobby buds atop 2' stems (these
can grow even taller in rich soils). Genuine wild forms of this species
are rare in commerce; the popular cultivar 'Whitleyi Major' probably
most closely represents its appearance in nature.

Hailing from the eastern Caucasus, *P. mlokosewitschii* is one of
the most coveted of peony species — as well as one of the more
snarling strings of syllables in the plant world. Though known
commonly as "Mollie the Witch," I find the specific epithet

Paeonia cambessedesii

Paeonia tenuifolia

(muh-law-ko-zuh-VEE-chee-eye), once mastered, much more eu-
phonious. In mid- to late spring, its exquisite orbs of glistening,
soft sulphur — held above handsome, 2'-tall mounds of grayish
green, felted foliage — barely open before shattering. Even though
its period of floral interest is only a few days, my plants always

Paeonia mlokosewitschii

thrives in the light shade of deciduous trees as well as in open alpine meadows. It is a grand plant in cultivation, producing capacious mounds of glossy green foliage rising to 2.5'. The flowers appear on sturdy 3' stems, with a shape similar to *P. mlokosewitschii* though they are much paler, with just a tinge of yellow, contrasting with rusty red pistils. Later, the flowers give rise to superb fruit.

Quite a number of species, in fact, produce unexpectedly colorful fruit. Shining examples include *P. japonica* and *P. obovata*. The former, native to Japan and Korea, offers a short season of frosty white, yellow-centered flowers on 15" stems, followed by the standard turquoise-blue gems within a scarlet-lined follicle. I have seen *P. japonica* in South Korea growing amid colonies of bamboo in very shaded sites, and so I cultivate my collections of this species in our woodland garden, where it thrives. Although British plantsman Graham Stuart Thomas declares that it "will not set the Thames on fire," I find its understated charm reason enough to cultivate it.

Paeonia obovata is better known and more frequently sought in its pure white form, *P. obovata* var. *alba*, but I consider the more common soft-pink-flowered form equally desirable. Native from Manchuria to eastern Russia, it combines a hardy constitution with pure elegance of flower. Globes of tightly incurved petals atop 20" stems appear in late spring, resulting later in spectacular crops of fruit. Although best suited to full sun in well-drained soil, it thrives in a bright location in our woodland.

Flower and fruit do not constitute the only attractions of the

set quantities of sapphire-blue seeds held within a scarlet-lined purse that last for many weeks — ample recompense for the brevity of blossom.

Of similar overall appearance, *P. wittmanniana* occurs naturally from the western Caucasus to the Iranian Plateau, where it wild peony, however. For many species, particularly those with such fleeting bloom, the lion's share of seasonal effect comes from foliage, which can be sensational. One of the earliest-blooming herbaceous species in my garden is *P. cambessedesii* (Zone 8), native to the islands of the Mediterranean. In late March, its diminutive leaves appear, with a lovely metallic blue gleam on the upper surface and a ruby-burnished undersurface. Shortly thereafter, the single, rich pink flowers emerge, with their carmine marbling and large boss of golden anthers. The foliage brings to mind a good form of *Helleborus foetidus*, which is not particularly surprising when one considers that both are members of the buttercup family (Ranunculaceae).

In fact, when the floral season of *P. veitchii* is upon us in our garden, visitors often ask, "What is that lovely, nodding pink hellebore that is blooming so late?" It is indeed enchanting in flower, yet I have come to appreciate this species, from the mountains of China's Sichuan Province, mostly for its smashingly good foliage. Deeply cut, fingery leaves of bright green remain handsome throughout the summer, long after the flowers depart. *Paeonia anomala* is similar, with deeper, more saturated flowers of crimson. Though considered by some to be sturdier than *P. veitchii*, that has not been my experience.

Supreme in regard to foliage is *P. tenuifolia*, a native of the high, stony mountains of the central Caucasus. This species bears magnificent, 15" mounds of finely fretted leaves that form a veritable chlorophyllous cloud, a top-notch foil to the single, blood-red

flowers centered with a tuft of flaxen stamens. The double-flowered form of this species, 'Plena', is locally more abundant than the single form, and though I often shy away from such unnatural loveliness, I have to admit that I find it a better garden plant altogether.

I would be remiss not to at least mention our native peony species, which inhabit the eastern slopes of the Cascades and the Coastal Ranges of Southern California. *Paeonia brownii* thrives on high, arid slopes from Washington to Nevada, producing demure, nodding flowers of ruddy maroon on 8" stems. Similar in effect is *P. californica*, with subdued flowers of sooty red. While both are considered difficult in a garden setting, it is nevertheless troubling that they are so often overlooked within our natural heritage.

Woody Species

Of course, not all peony species retreat to ground level when winter arrives. The woody species of *Paeonia*, however, pose a formidable challenge to the taxonomist. Not only have their origins and behavior in the wild been vastly understudied; they also occur only within the confines of Tibet and China, an immense area whose borders have periodically closed and reopened over the centuries. Add to this isolation the aura of veneration that surrounds them in their native country, and the hazards of peony nomenclature become apparent.

Though nearly all of the shrubby species of peony offered for sale in the United States are designated as cultivars of *P. suffruticosa*, in all likelihood they represent complex hybrids between numerous species. One exception is the famously expensive *P. rockii*, which for years went by the name of *P. suffruticosa* 'Rock's Variety' or 'Joseph Rock', but has recently been elevated to what is known in botany as "specific rank." The immense flowers of this species are indeed incredible: borne on sturdy, 5' stems, they consist of numerous rows of pure white petals that startle to deep burgundy at the base. Is the plant worth $150 a crack? Every penny.

With my colleagues, I have collected seeds of *P. delavayi* from the dry, high-elevation slopes and plateaus of Yunnan Province in western China. In early spring, *P. delavayi* produces stunning sable flowers with burgundy overtones on stems to 3', set off by handsome, pinnate, bluish green foliage. Natural populations of this species contain individuals with flowers ranging from near black to clear lemon yellow (in *P. delavayi* var. *lutea*), with a delicious assortment of intermediate shades.

Paeonia obovata var. *alba*

Paeonia cambessedesii, fruit

Paeonia delavayi

The cultivation of most species peony is precisely like that of their more thoroughbred progeny. (The exceptions are the American species, which are best grown in cool, arid climates in very well drained soil.) They respond best to autumn planting to allow for sufficient root establishment before top growth begins in spring. Choose a site in full sun, or in partial shade for those species that prefer woodland conditions. Amend the soil with aged compost, and keep any heavy mulch away from the crown of the plant. Add 1 lb. of bone meal per plant at planting time and every autumn thereafter. Blind (i.e., nonflowering) stems will often develop on peonies that have been planted too deeply; the "eyes," or buds, should be buried no deeper than 1" to 2".

To reduce the risk of botrytis, remove the spent foliage and discard it — do not add it to the compost pile. In the words of my friend, Les Brake, a superb gardener from Willow, Alaska, and peony cultivator extraordinaire, "Gardening is like religion; whatever you believe works."

More robust is *P. ludlowii*, which hails from the Tibetan Plateau. The sand-colored stems of this species can reach 8' in cultivation, and carry handsome pinnate foliage and multitudes of rich yellow flowers in May. Autumn can bring a second show, with buttery yellow foliage held by petioles that intensify to pinkish violet.

And what of the "true" *P. suffruticosa*? I have it growing in my garden from seed collected in the wild, though it is years away from its first blossoming. I'm simply hoping for an unpretentious, basic flower; in the meantime, I don't intend to worry about its taxonomic status — better botanists than I will have the mess adequately sorted out before my fledgling finally flowers.

The complete story of the genus *Paeonia* is much more complex, of course. How can one possibly choose from such an aristocratic assemblage? And how can one find the perfect adjective to describe the first thrust of peony foliage through the thawing earth of early spring, the promise of swollen buds, or those precise, silken flowers? Perhaps it is best to close with the words of Reginald Farrer, a feisty, early-20th-century British gardener and plantsman who perfectly understood the essence of the wild peony: "Let all those [peonies] that are too wild and small to cope with the bloated beauties of the border, have their acknowledged place in the garden, in some fitting corner of deep hollow or high cool ledge."

CREAM OF THE CRANESBILLS

an expert picks the best hardy geraniums

by DANIEL J. HINKLEY

I find it difficult now to remember how I first came to know the hardy geraniums.

It may have been through the low carpet of *Geranium sanguineum* var. *lancastriense*, with its upturned flowers of soft pink etched with rose, that has long been a feature in my garden. Or perhaps the loud magenta-flowered *G. psilostemon* first caught my attention. Whatever the plant responsible for my initial infatuation, I have since acquired a large number of these durable and charming perennials, which have become an indispensable component of my borders. Now, with a decade of geranium growing behind me, I sometimes wonder which species and cultivars I would most want to keep if, for some reason, I were made to choose. It's a difficult decision, for new and better hybrids are constantly being introduced. I have come to realize,

however, that among this confusing welter there already exist a great number of hardy geraniums with timeless qualities.

Classic Cranesbills

Etched in my memory is an early-March scene at Hidcote Manor in England: snow squalls suddenly swept in on the garden where vast stands of *Geranium macrorrhizum* were in lush early growth, leaving each leaf surrounded by the icy white of newly fallen snow. This surprisingly tough species brings freshness to the early-spring garden unequaled by any other plant. *Geranium macrorrhizum* (hardy to USDA Zone 3) produces robust clumps of thick, fleshy stems bearing lobed,

Geranium 'Spinners'

felted, 4" leaves that are distinctively pine-scented and 1" flowers in various shades from eye-popping magenta to nearly white. There are several familiar selections, such as 'Bevan's Variety', 'Spessart', and 'Ingwersen's Variety', though plants sold under these names are often incorrectly identified. Hardy geraniums have a propensity to self-sow directly into the parent clump, resulting in imposters that are inadvertently passed along under the parent plant's name. In fact, I suspect that these older cultivars are extinct and are represented today by seedlings that simply fit their descriptions.

Fortunately, some of the newer selections are ample compensation for the older cultivars. *Geranium macrorrhizum* 'Czakor' produces 15" mounds of foliage and an early display of highly charged magenta blossoms that are particularly striking when grown near the lime-green croziers of unfurling ferns. It might aptly be described as a more intensely colored form of 'Bevan's Variety'. The same may be said of *G. m.* 'Pindus', originally found in the wilds of Greece, with similarly bright flowers on dense, 8" mounds of foliage. Search long and hard enough, and you will find a variegated form of any plant, and *G. macrorrhizum* is no exception. *Geranium macrorrhizum* 'Variegatum' produces creamily marbled, pinkish-stained foliage that slowly forms a handsome clump. Slowly is the operative word here, for this selection is exasperatingly touchy and must be given supplemental moisture and fertilizer if it is not to look like one of the garden's casualties. The rich rose flowers are infrequently produced, though in this case the gorgeous foliage makes them superfluous.

Geranium macrorrhizum 'Czakor'

Groundcovers and Ramblers

Geranium phaeum (Zone 5; 1.5'–2.5') and its many cultivars are as effective when used as groundcover, especially in areas of dry shade, as when used as single specimens in the mixed border. Commonly known as mourning widow for its somber, bruise-colored flowers with strongly flaring petals, it also bears interesting foliage, its dark green, rounded leaves marked with blackish purple. A seedling found in the wild by former nurserywoman Elizabeth Strangman has foliage with a broad band of purple, resembling a zonal pelargonium. Named for the village near where it was found, 'Samobor' is one of the most striking foliage plants to come on the scene for some time. In full sun, it combines remarkably well with the bright golden foliage of *Philadelphus coronarius* 'Aureus'; in partial shade, try it with the gilded foliage of *Filipendula ulmaria* 'Aurea' and *Hosta* 'Sun Power'.

Two white-variegated forms of this species — *G. phaeum* 'Variegatum' and *G. p.* 'Taff's Jester' — enliven plantings of ferns, arisaemas and hostas in my woodland garden. The former, which made the rounds for many years under the misnomer 'Muldoon', has irregularly blotched white and green foliage with random streaks of coral and plum. The leaves look as though they have caught and held the rays of sun broken by the limbs of the Douglas firs growing above. 'Taff's Jester' begins the season with leaves suffused with whitish gold, fading to frosted green as the season progresses. It looks superb in semishade paired with early bluebells.

Geranium phaeum shows remarkable variation in flowers as well as foliage, much to the gardener's benefit. 'Joan Baker' produces copious quantities of reflexed, grayish lavender blossoms on 15" stems above luscious clumps of green foliage. Its refined color combines wonderfully with the platinum filigree of artemisias or, in a container with the tender, silver-foliaged morning glory *Convolvulus cneorum. Geranium phaeum* 'Album', with pure white flowers held above mounds of bright green foliage, is one of my favorite cranesbills for woodland conditions. In late April in my garden, the flowers of this selection mingle with the dark purple sepals of an exceptionally long-lasting hybrid hellebore (*Helleborus* ×*hybridus*), bridging the gap between winter and summer. A third cultivar, 'Lily Lovell', boasts the richest color of all, with deep grape-purple flowers held on upright stems above lush mounds of deep green foliage.

Geranium pratense 'Victor Reiter'

isons of this plant to the better-known *G. sylvaticum* 'Mayflower' showed it was indeed superior, and we subsequently named it 'Nikita', in our dog's memory. It is *G. sylvaticum* 'Amy Doncaster', however, that takes top billing among selections of this species. I had the luck to meet the outstanding plantswoman for whom this geranium was named at a nursing home in the south of England, shortly before her death at the age of 100. As we talked, the names of plants brought back images of her once-famous garden, and her eyes lit up with pure joy. 'Amy Doncaster' bears deep blue flowers without a hint of lavender, centered with pure white, produced atop 15" bright green mounds of foliage in early summer. I have this lovely selection at the base of a weeping larch so that the blue flowers can consort with the bright spring-green needles on the larch's lowest branches.

The felted, pewter-gray foliage of *G. renardii* (Zone 4; 1'), held in handsome, ever-expanding clumps, is among the loveliest of any cranesbill, which is a good thing, considering that the whitish lavender flowers are a dingy disappointment. For the sake of the foliage alone, however, I would never be without this species. Moreover, it will grow in a hot, baking position and poor soil as well as in richer soil and semishade. I use *G. renardii* as a low groundcover flanking the gray paving stone in our mixed border, where it both echoes the color of the stone and serves as an outstanding foil to the dwarf, sanguine spikes of *Sanguisorba* 'Tanna', which blooms nearby throughout the summer.

It is unsurpassed for smothering weeds, and looks splendid when contrasted with the bright foliage of the elderberry *Sambucus racemosa* 'Sutherland Gold'.

Geranium sylvaticum (Zones 5; 1'–2'), native to open woodlands in Europe and Turkey, is a superb species for floral effect. From crowded clusters of nodding buds, the flowers open and turn upward in long progression. The distinctive broad, lobed leaves are hardly less handsome. A chance seedling of this species with rounded, deep lavender petals occurred in our garden not far from where we had recently buried our cocker spaniel. Compar-

Recently, *G. renardii* has crossed with the robust, violet-flowered species *G. platypetalum* to produce *G.* 'Phillipe Vapelle' (Zones 5; 10"–12"), a plant that possesses the same desirable foliage of *G. renardii* with the bonus of attractive flowers in deep shades of lavender. Another cross between *Geranium renardii* and the Turkish species *G. gracile* gave rise to a handsome hybrid known as *G.* 'Chantilly' (Zone 5; 12"), whose felted, lobed, bright green foliage is midway between its two parents. *Geranium gracile*, which demands abundant moisture to perform well, may have had another unintended effect on 'Chantilly', for the handsome foliage will often burn in full sun and hot positions. In rich, moist soils or in light shade, however, the foliage forms a superb backdrop to the pinkish lavender flowers, which are produced in abundance throughout the summer.

Exciting Sun Lovers

Geranium procurrens (Zone 5; 4") is a Himalayan species that, as its specific epithet implies, can procure large areas of the garden in a single season. Its tendency to root and run can be corralled by planting it at the base of shrubs; that way, its wandering stems can climb up into the shrubs' branches, where they will unfold their dark-eyed purple flowers in summer. Matrimony with other species has tamed *G. procurrens*'s wandering ways, resulting in even better garden plants. Perhaps the best known of the lot is *G.* 'Ann Folkard' (Zone 5), the result of a union with *G. psilostemon*. Trailing stems as long as 6' clad with chartreuse foliage emerge from the plant's crown to explore the garden in every direction, but retreat at season's end to their point of origin. Throughout the summer the plant puts on a nonstop display of large,

black-eyed magenta flowers. A sister seedling from the same cross, 'Anne Thomson' (Zone 5), has nearly identical flowers and foliage but forms a 15" clump. Both are extremely useful in combination with purple-foliaged shrubs and perennials, such as *Berberis thunbergii* 'Atropurpurea', *Cotinus coggygria* Purpureus Group or *Euphorbia dulcis* 'Chameleon'.

Paired with *G. lambertii*, a species with large, rose flowers richly veined in pink, *G. procurrens* has given rise to the spectacular late-blooming hybrid 'Salome' (Zone 6; 6"), with intense yellow foliage and flowers of deep rose veined with purple that becomes more noticeable in the center. It is superlative in full sun planted near the dark violet bracts and steely blue leaves of the annual *Cerinthe major* 'Purpurascens'.

Double cranesbills provide outstanding value in the border. Because the flowers are sterile, the plants do not expend energy in producing seed, and thus the flowering season extends throughout most of the summer months. Some of the most attractive doubles can be a challenge to find, but I can attest that they are well worth

Geranium pratense 'Plenum Violaceum'

the effort. *Geranium pratense* (Zone 4; 2'–3'), common in meadows throughout northern Europe, offers three outstanding double forms: 'Plenu Caeruleum', which bears large, double, lavender flowers suffused with light blue on 2' stems. Over time, it makes a robust clump and will benefit from regular division. In a large, sunny island bed in our backyard, this cultivar pairs magnificently with the pewter filigree foliage of *Artemisia* 'Powis Castle'.

A number of single forms of *Geranium pratense* also make welcome additions to the early-summer garden, whether in the precisely planted herbaceous border or more freely designed informal settings. *Geranium p.* 'Mrs. Kendall Clark', a lovely strain that comes true from seed, possesses flowers of an intriguing silvery lavender veined in a deeper hue. *Geranium p.* 'Silver Queen' sports

Geranium 'Ann Folkard'

shimmering pink flowers with darker veins and produces robust clumps best suited to the midborder. It comes reasonably true from seed but is better if divided. A single plant of *G. p.* 'Striatum' can simultaneously produce flowers that are pure white, lavender blue and streaked and spotted with both colors. Its offspring can be kept true to form by discarding any seedlings with pinkish leaf petioles.

Though I may be at risk of overselling cranesbills with outstanding foliage, I cannot pass over the colored-leaf forms of *G. pratense*. There are two, both variations on a plum-purple theme. 'Victor Reiter' turned up in the early 1970s in the garden of a San Franciscan nurseryman of the same name. The finely dissected leaves emerge with a deep violet suffusion in early spring and mature to forest green with a purplish blush. Throughout early summer, rich lavender-blue flowers appear nearly nonstop. When the plant is grown in isolation, or when the flowers are hand-pollinated, one-quarter of the progeny revert to the standard green-leaved form of the species, one-half resemble the parent, and

one-quarter emerge with extremely dark purple foliage as dusky as a Kansas thundercloud. The latter strain is currently available under the name *G. p.* Midnight Reiter strain. The plant's only failing is that it takes a relatively long time to form a sizable clump. I have used this plant to good effect in full sun with the upright white-and-green spears of *Sisyrinchium striatum* 'Aunt May' and the rich pink, spurred flowers of *Diascia* 'Wendy'. As the availability of Midnight Reiter strain increases, it is only a matter of time before new crosses are made that take its superb foliage to new heights.

All the forms of *G. pratense* may suffer from a midsummer infection of powdery mildew that can be remedied by a quick and painless crewcut once flowering is over. The new foliage will not only be resistant to infection but will provide fresh greenery for the rest of the summer.

One of my favorite hardy geraniums has *G. pratense* as one of its parents. (The other has yet to admit responsibility.) The history of

Geranium phaeum 'Variegatum'

this hybrid is associated with the late Marvin Black, who was arborist for the city of Seattle before his death in 1987. Black had sent seed of *G. pratense* to Spinners Nursery, near Southampton in England. There the proprietor, Peter Chappell, sowed the seed and selected from the resulting seedlings one with superb, deeply dissected foliage and outstanding vigor. Named 'Spinners' (Zone 4), it grew into a plant that produces remarkable quantities of large, cuplike, bluish lavender flowers all summer long from mounds of foliage that rise to 4' by summer's end. Though it makes an outstanding addition to almost any summer floral scheme, I have enjoyed it most planted near a simple wooden garden bench

in our garden. By late summer, its wandering strands of flower and leaf have woven themselves above and through the bench's bleached slats, making it nearly impossible to sit, but creating a stunning spectacle.

Exploring the vast genus *Geranium* may be exhausting, but it is also an exhilarating adventure, one that can yield the perfect plant for almost every part of the garden. If the prospect seems daunting, then we simply need to make the journey one plant at a time, taking comfort in the knowledge that there is always another wonderful hardy geranium waiting to be discovered.

DAISIES THAT DAZZLE

with their immense clusters of sumptuously colored flowers, heleniums bring summer's warmth to the early-fall border

by THOMAS FISCHER

"Oh no," I can hear you groan, "please, not more daisies." Believe me, I sympathize. By this point in the gardening year, you've had to endure wave after wave of perky, nearly indistinguishable composites — coreopsis, heliopsis, helianthus, inulas, silphiums and Lord knows what else.

Trust me, though — heleniums are different. First of all, there's the shape of the flowers. Yes, they do follow the familiar composite pattern of a circular cluster of short disk florets surrounded by elongated, brightly colored ray florets (the petals). But a helenium's disk florets form a kind of rounded knob — *subglobose* is the technical adjective — that transforms the flower from your typical two-dimensional daisy into something much more interesting and sculptural, while the ray florets (in most varieties), instead of being long and narrow, are short and notched, giving each flower head a trim, elegant look.

Helenium 'Feuersiegel'

Helenium 'Kupferzwerg'

Helenium 'Waltraut'

Then there are the warm, toasty colors, which strike a harmonious seasonal chord. (Although a few of these robust, hardy — to USDA Zone 3 in most cases — perennials bloom as early as June and July, most wait until August or September.) Sure, there are plenty of yellow-flowered species and hybrids, but there are also deep, smoldering reds, coppery browns and rich, warm oranges — colors that make you think of sandstone canyons or Mexican *mole* sauces. There are even selections in whose ray florets two or more colors blend in hallucinatory swirls, or in which an underlying color is washed and stippled with a contrasting hue. Exciting enough for you?

Origins

The genus *Helenium* contains upwards of 40 perennial and annual species, all of them native to the New World; only a handful, however,

have made the leap from the wild to the garden. (Their common name of sneezeweed, by the way, not only grates on the ear, it is also inaccurate, since heleniums are not in the least allergy-provoking, a fact I confirmed by means of a simple experiment involving my highly allergic co-gardener. All in the interests of science, of course.) Of these 40, the most important is the highly variable perennial *H. autumnale*, an inhabitant of moist soils over a huge stretch of North America, from Quebec to British Columbia and from Florida to Arizona. Growing anywhere from 2' to 5', it bears narrow, toothed leaves and 1"- to 2"-wide deep yellow flowers. Its horticultural significance derives not from its own fairly modest charms, but rather from its status as the primary ancestor of the dozens of opulent hybrids currently available; in its various wild forms, *H. autumnale* is likely to appeal only to the most die-hard native-plant enthusiasts.

There are at least two other perennial species, though, that are attractive enough for border use. *Helenium hoopesii*, native to the Rocky Mountains west to Oregon and California, grows from 2' to 3' tall and bears 3", deep yellow-orange flowers with straplike, slightly drooping rays in late May or early June — exceptionally early for a helenium. The foliage is distinct as well, being gray green, entire (that is, untoothed), and with individual leaves up to 1' long.

The other is *H. bigelovii*, a West Coast species most often encountered in the selection called 'The Bishop'. Whereas the wild form of *H. bigelovii* can grow as tall as four feet, 'The Bishop' stays a compact 28" and sports short, deep yellow rays surrounding a blackish-brown center. Most references list *H. bigelovii* as being much less hardy than other heleniums — only to Zone 6 or 7 —

Helenium 'Moerheim Beauty' with *Crocosmia ×crocosmiiflora*

but I suspect this is a case of limited anecdotal information getting passed from book to book without confirmation from gardeners who have actually grown the plant.

Hybrids

Pleasant as *H. hoopesii* and *H. bigelovii* may be, it's the hybrids that really get your juices flowing. As with the Michaelmas daisies, border phlox and bedding penstemons, here again we have the case of a group of plain American wildflowers crossing the Atlantic and coming back fancy. Whether you consider the changes to be an improvement or a corruption depends, I suppose, on how you feel about "improved" flowers in general. Personally, I don't see how anyone can object when the result is a wider palette of more vivid colors, a longer bloom period and a sturdier overall constitution, but then I've always been a fan of artifice.

Although the British have contributed a modest number of hybrids (Blooms of Bressingham's coppery red 'Coppelia', for example), the majority have originated in Continental nurseries, particularly in Germany and the Netherlands. Among the Olympians of helenium breeding, the preeminent figure is the German nurseryman Karl Foerster, who, over a career spanning more than six decades, released some 73 cultivars remarkable for their vigor, large flowers and tolerance of (relatively) drier soil. Sadly, most of Foerster's selections have disappeared over the years, but some are still available, including 'Goldrausch', 'Kanaria', 'Königstiger', 'Zimbelstern', and my favorite, the brownish orange 'Septemberfuchs'. Only slightly less venerable is Foerster's countryman, Gustav Deutschmann, who has given us 'Baudirektor Linne', 'Waltraut', and the admirably compact 'Kupferzwerg' and 'Rubinzwerg', the latter a true gem in rich, dark reddish brown. Among Dutch breeders, Bonne Ruys deserves mention for his classic, reddish bronze 'Moerheim Beauty', an early bloomer that

Helenium hoopesii

will reflower later in the season if scrupulously deadheaded. With luck (and a bit of prompting), American nurseries will soon start importing the sturdy new plants of another Dutch breeder, Inez Arnold, whose hybrids include the bicolor, gaillardia-like 'Gay-Go-Round' and 'Ring of Fire', the sumptuous crimson-brown 'Potter's Wheel', and the yellow, large-flowered 'Summer Circle'.

Care and Cultivation

Heleniums aren't fussy plants, but neither are they the sort of perennial you can just stick in the ground and forget about. They need full sun and fertile soil for strong growth and abundant bloom, and a reasonably steady supply of moisture. (Although, as I mentioned above, the Foerster hybrids are able to tolerate occasional dryness, xeric they aren't.) This means they will need to be fed in spring when they are coming into growth, either with the organic matter of your choice (compost, rotted manure) or a fertilizer with a slightly elevated phosphorus ratio, and that they will need to be watered in dry spells. Thus cared for, they can stay put for many years. If your plants start to look spindly, however, you'll need to divide them in early spring and replant the divisions in enriched soil.

It pains me to admit it, but heleniums produce such massive heads of flowers that some of the taller cultivars need to be staked to prevent them from flopping. If staking is a chore you can't or won't deal with, you can simply limit yourself to those selections (especially those cultivars whose names end in –zwerg, the German word for dwarf) that top off at 2' to 3'. Another way to solve the flopping problem is to pinch back the new growth by half in late spring, which will produce shorter, sturdier plants (but will also delay flowering by a couple of weeks).

Using Heleniums in the Border

In my own garden I've found that heleniums combine brilliantly with just about anything in the deep blue or purple range — for example asters ('Veilchenkönigin' and 'Violetta'), monkshoods, leadwort (Ceratostigma plumbaginoides) and delphiniums in their second blooming — but this is hardly an original discovery. Way back when, Gertrude Jekyll used big drifts of what she called Helenium pumilum (probably a dwarf, early-blooming form of H. autumnale) in the blue, yellow and white border she designed for the garden at Presaddfed in northern Wales. Here, the blues come mainly from delphiniums, Anchusa azurea and Salvia patens; the whites from snapdragons, foxgloves and Clematis recta; and the other yellows from achilleas, coreopsis, marigolds, oenotheras, snapdragons and rudbeckias. Very zingy.

Another possibility occurs to me. If some people can have an aster border (a certain domestic goddess and media mogul comes to mind), why not a helenium border? Besides a generous assortment of heleniums in yellow, orange, red and brown, it would need, I think, lots of grasses — selections of miscanthus (especially stripy cultivars like 'Strictus' and 'Goldfeder'), calamagrostis (C. ×acutiflora 'Karl Foerster', appropriately), Stipa tenuissima, and maybe even some of the bronze carexes, if your climate is mild enough. Then how about tossing in some late-blooming kniphofias (perhaps 'Bressingham Comet' or 'Cobra'), some goldenrods, bronze fennel and a scattering of Lilium henryi? You can practically feel the heat.

facts and FIGURES

TYPE OF PLANT: herbaceous perennial **FAMILY:** Asteraceae (daisy family) **HEIGHT:** 24"–60", depending on cultivar **LEAVES:** 1" wide to 6" long, lanceolate, usually lightly serrate, medium green **FLOWERS:** individual flowers to 2" across, borne in dense clusters, yellow through orange to reddish brown **BLOOM PERIOD:** June–September, depending on cultivar **HARDINESS:** USDA Zones 3–8 (most varieties) **EXPOSURE:** full sun **SOIL:** fertile, well-drained **WATER NEEDS:** moderately high **FEEDING:** once annually in early spring with compost, composted manure or a fertilizer formulated for flowering perennials **PROPAGATION:** by division in spring **PROBLEMS:** none serious; taller cultivars may need staking

Helenium 'Pumilum Magnificum'

HELENIUMS AT A GLANCE

SPECIES OR CULTIVAR	HEIGHT	BLOOM PERIOD	DESCRIPTION
H. bigelovii 'The Bishop'	28"	middle	large, deep yellow flowers, black disk
H. hoopesii	24"–36"	very early	large, yellow-orange flowers on strong stems; tolerates dry soil
'Baudirektor Linne'	38"–42"	late	velvety red brown with dark brown disk, long-lasting
'Blütentisch'	32"–38"	middle	golden yellow, reverse marked red brown, brown disk, arching habit
'Bruno'	38"–42"	middle	dark mahogany red, flower somewhat uneven
'Butterpat'	38"	late	deep yellow flowers, yellow-green disk
'Coppelia'	38"	middle	swirled coppery red, fades to burnt orange, dark red-brown disk
'Feuersiegel'	36"–42"	late	deep red flowers edged with yellow, yellow circle around light brown disk
'Goldrausch'	48"–60"	late	golden yellow marked with brown, green-brown disk, very free-flowering
'Kanaria'	42"–46"	middle	bright yellow flowers, formal in shape, green-yellow disk
'Königstiger'	42" to 46"	middle	golden yellow flowers with dark red-brown margin, petals uneven
'Kupfersprudel'	42"–46"	middle	coppery brown flowers streaked with yellow, dark brown disk
'Kupferzwerg'	24"	late	orange-red flowers, brown disk
'Moerheim Beauty'	28"–32"	early	rich brownish red flowers, fade to warm brown, dark disk
'Pumilum Magnificum'	28"	early–middle	golden yellow with red-brown base, dark yellow disk
'Rubinzwerg'	28"	middle	very rich red brown, dark reddish brown disk
'Septemberfuchs'	48"–60"	late	red brown overlaid on yellow, looks light orange brown, smallish flowers
'Waltraut'	32"–36"	early	golden brown marked with yellow; very large flower heads
'Zimbelstern'	48"–60"	middle	deep gold flowers washed with tawny brown, disk dark brown

*early = June–July; middle = July–August; late = August–September

Most heleniums are hardy in USDA Zones 3–8, though many sources list 'The Bishop' as hardy only to Zone 6.

MINTS WITH A TWIST

These little-known members of a well-known family offer dazzling flowers and handsome foliage

by LAUREN SPRINGER

While struggling with plant taxonomy in college, I was relieved to find the mint family, or Lamiaceae, easy to remember. Unlike many botanical families, which require contrived mnemonics to summon up during an identification exam, the labiates' characteristic square stems and four-ranked leaf arrangement are unmistakable. The pungently fragrant foliage of many species offers olfactory cues. What's more, the irregularly shaped flowers evoke petulant mouths with protruding lower "lips" (labia in Latin), hence the family name.

This large, cosmopolitan family includes hundreds of perennials, annuals and small shrubs for the garden with a diversity of color, texture and scent that few other groups can rival. As an East Coaster, my first horticultural encounters with this family were limited to a few well-known herbs and a handful of lanky, late-blooming tender salvias and agastaches from south of the border. Now a sun-dried, wind-worn denizen of northern Colorado, I have discovered unsung labiate genera such as *Dracocephalum*, *Marrubium*, *Phlomis*, *Scutellaria* and *Sideritis*. These beautiful yet tough plants have proven themselves ideally adapted to the rigors of the North American high plains climate. All of the plants mentioned here are hardy in my garden, having survived temperatures ranging from −33°F to 105°F. In milder regions, they can be enjoyed on well-drained, sloped sites, in rock walls and as welcome additions to herb and Mediterranean-style gardens. Some are obscure plants grown only by rock gardeners, others are new twists on tried-and-true border perennials, and a large number are recent introductions from Turkey and central Asia.

Labiates for the Border

In an English-inspired mixed border of old garden roses and perennials, mint-family members add spiky variety and contrast to the softer, more voluptuous curves of the roses. Among the more robust and architectural are members of the genus *Phlomis*, with their tiered whorls of hooded flowers. Butter yellow *P. russeliana* (to 2'), with large, handsome, felted green leaves, sets off to perfection smoky red-purple roses such as the *gallica* 'Cardinal de Richelieu'. *Phlomis cashmeriana*, also about 2' tall but with a more slender silhouette, has grayer foliage and lavender-pink flowers. *Phlomis samia*, often thought to be identical to *P. russeliana*, is actually quite distinct, with tawny flowers speckled in

Agastache barberi

purple, and foliage covered by an animal-like, biscuit-colored indumentum.

Outstanding at the front of the border are two nonflowering forms of that old favorite, lamb's ears. *Stachys byzantina* 'Silver Carpet' is aptly named; *S. b.* 'Big Ears' has larger leaves that are more of a sage green. Two other species to grow for both their flowers and crimped, deep green foliage are *S. nivea*, creamy white in bloom, and *S. densiflora* (also known as *S. monieri*), with deep rose-pink flowers. Less than 1' in height, they bloom in late spring, and are lovely at the base of black-purple bearded irises such as 'Superstition'.

In midsummer, the biennial clary sage (*Salvia sclarea*) expands

its pungent, 4'-tall floral candelabra. The opalescent pink bracts remain attractive for a good month after the actual blossoms have faded. *Salvia sclarea* var. *turkestanica*, a perennial form of this sage, thrives in the hottest sun as well as in light, dry shade, where it marries well with lemon-yellow daylilies. On the heels of clary sage come the rich lavender spikes of 2'-tall *Salvia verticillata*, which I prefer to the popular *S. ×superba*. Not only does *S. verticillata* flower at a needier time in the garden — late July — but it also has large, hairy, gray-green leaves that look good before, during and after the floral display, while *S. ×superba*'s undistinguished foliage becomes a tatty mess after bloom. Although a white form of *S. verticillata* can be had, I rely on the extra-deep hue of the cultivar 'Purple Rain' to hold up against the bleaching Colorado sun. It makes a smoldering pair with red *Verbena peruviana*.

The border season finishes with a few members of the agastache clan. Like Salvia, this genus contains many heat-loving tender beauties that don't begin to bloom until about two days before our first frost. Others, such as the common *A. foeniculum*, are frumpy things whose only appeal is fragrant foliage and the butterflies they attract. Fortunately, several hardy, long-blooming, fragrant, beautiful species exist that also draw their share of bees, butterflies and hummingbirds. The candy-pink southwestern native *A. cana* has been dubbed the "Double Bubble Mint" for its strong, sweet fragrance. (Even the seeds smell good; my mouth watered while I was sowing them.) Its small, sage-green foliage is topped with stout flower spikes reaching 2'. Its close relative *A. pallidiflora* subsp. *pallidiflora* (also known as *A. barberi*) is1' or so taller and begins flowering a bit earlier. Its foliage is less gray green; on some individuals it is suffused with purple. Both agastaches bloom well into September. Orange, long the pariah of garden colors, gets a reprieve in autumn when even the most devout pastel devotees often give it a chance. 15"-tall *A. rupestris* and 2' *A. aurantiaca* are both orange-flowered, airy, late-season beauties. The former is more peach in tone, with wispy gray foliage; the latter's tubular flowers are bicolored in sunset hues of orange and purple. Both are sublime with the lavender heath aster selection 'Ringdove' or with the larger lilac daisies of *Aster ×frikartii*.

Labiates for Light Shade

Most labiates come from sunny climes the world over, and therefore are not shade-lovers. A few, however, do admirably well with less than a full day's sun, and their drought tolerance makes them a valuable asset for that dreaded set of conditions, dry shade. In cloudy regions, these plants thrive out in the open, but the relentless 300-plus days of sun that sear a good third of continental North America are too much for them. One such species is a tame relative of that groundcovering delinquent, *Ajuga reptans*. *Ajuga chamaepitys* sprawls on the ground, spreading a bit, but is so threadlike and fine-textured, with finely dissected, hairy, gray-green foliage beneath its yellow flowers, that it can hardly be called invasive. It pops up discreetly between other plants, never running them over like its ill-mannered cousin. In early summer, 15"-tall *Stachys grandiflora* blooms with the showiest flowers of its genus. The flower spikes, rose pink or more rarely white, rise above a dense green clump of scalloped foliage, a good companion to pale columbines. Cut-leaf self-heal, *Prunella vulgaris* 'Laciniata', offers a 1'-

tall mound of deeply incised, somber, plum-tinted foliage to contrast with vivid pink flowers.

Most woodland salvias are coarse and weedy, but *Salvia forsskaolii*, although an energetic self-sower, has handsome rugose foliage and long-lasting, 2' spires of large, navy-blue flowers for many weeks beginning in early summer. Then come the shrimplike oreganos, so often considered sun-loving plants but actually ideally suited to dry, cool, light shade reminiscent of the north-facing slopes they inhabit in the wild. Their chartreuse bracts enclose white, lavender or rose flowers. In the case of petite *Origanum amanum* or purple-tinted *O. laevigatum*, the flowers draw most of the attention, while with *O. libanoticum*, *O. rotundifolium*, and *O. acutidens* the bracts steal the show. All of these pair well with the magenta flowers of long-blooming labiate *Calamintha grandiflora*.

Tough Plants for the Hot, Dry Garden

I am a foliage and form snob; many of the more tractable rock garden plants have made their way into my garden on account of their leaves or overall shape. Harsh, windy, dry environments foster adaptations that make for architectural plants with striking foliage — cushions, subshrubs, evergreen mats, felted mounds, cascading billows.

Many of the hardy sages offer beautiful silver and gray foliage as well as good flowers, a far cry from the lax growth habit and plebeian leaves of their tender, fall-blooming relatives. *Salvia microstegia*, with furry, oak-shaped, gray-green leaves, bears handsome white inflorescences, superior to those of *S. aethiopsis*, which has

Salvia verticillata 'Purple Rain'

Stachys nivea

Stachys

become a weed in our region. *Salvia cyanescens* has foliage that is a dead ringer for lamb's-ears, but never becomes the fuzzy blob that *Stachys byzantina* can be after either a wet or a desiccating winter. Its sky-blue flowers are held aloft on 18", airy wands for two months in the summer, and it self-sows lightly. Last of the silvery salvias are two easily grown rock garden favorites: 10" mounding *S. pisidica*, with a long-lasting display of bicolor blue-and-white flowers, and tiny mat-forming *S. caespitosa*, with flowers of a more lavender blue.

Some of the best mint family members combine silver foliage with pale moonlight-yellow flowers. *Sideritis scardica* has thrived for almost a decade in my garden, making it one of the hardiest of this yellow-flowered genus. Its foliage is like a dwarf lamb's-ears; the luminescent yellow whorled flowers rise in dense 1' spikes. In bud, when they are at their most architectural, they are suffused with the palest lime green. Once open, they look like waxy tapers. Low-growing, white-leaved *Stachys chrysantha* and *S. iva* bear pale yellow flowers from late spring through most of the summer, lovely with the periwinkle-blue spikes and finely dissected, hairy gray-green foliage of *Salvia jurisicii*. Two skullcaps, *Scutellaria orientalis* and *S. supina*, offer good, green, fine-textured foliage and small but numerous pale yellow flowers resembling snapdragons. Their cascading habit and stature are similar to common catmint. In the evening, their flowers seem to glow long after the sun has set. They bloom for well over a month, and then, after a good deadheading, they flower again in late summer. Both make wonderful fillers between deeper and brighter colors, especially with the indigo biennial labiate *Dracocephalum nutans* and the showy, purple-bracted flower heads of *Salvia multicaulis*.

Two other skullcaps with exceptionally attractive flowers are the dark blue, mid- and late-summer-blooming *Scutellaria baicalensis*, at 15" a bit floppy, but gorgeous with orange butterfly weed, and the gray-leaved Great Plains native *S. resinosa*, with a tidy, shrubby, 10" habit and azure blue flowers.

The chartreuse velvet foliage of several horehounds is a soothing color in the harsh, drying sun at 5,000' above sea level. *Marrubium cylleneum*, with wavy leaf margins, and *M. rotundifolium*, whose orbicular foliage is rimmed in white, both have sprawling habits, while *M. friwaldskyanum* is more upright. In my garden, their soft color calms the cacophony of red, blue and lipstick-pink penstemon spikes. Intensely silver *M. incanum* and *M. candidissimum* have a stiffer habit. To look at them, you might think they were subshrubs of sorts; nevertheless, they are completely herbaceous in Colorado's fierce winters. Their upright silhouettes give a miniature

mixed-border effect. I use fragrant-leaved *Hyssopus officinalis* subsp. *aristatus* in the same role — its true-blue flowers, which come in late summer and are much favored by bees, are just an added bonus. Hyssop has deep green foliage, quite unusual among drought-tolerant plants, which adds a refreshing note to the many silvers and dusty gray-greens.

My favorite labiate of all is *Dracocephalum botryoides*. This beautiful dragonhead makes 4"-tall mats of gray-green, felted, scallop-edged evergreen foliage. In early spring, with the lipstick magenta cups of *Tulipa humilis* 'Persian Pearl' as companions, it sends forth rose-pink flower clusters embedded in fuzzy mauve calyxes.

As I venture into the garden on a wind-still winter's day, the warmth of the intense high-altitude sun allowing me to roll up my sleeves, one of the labiate family's most pleasant legacies invites me to continue my garden cleanup. As I cut back shrubby hyssop, lavender and straggly tangles of thymes, their delicious fragrances fill the sun-warmed air. Whether in the form of catnip to craze a feline, nectar and pollen for myriad bees, butterflies and hummingbirds, or the foliage of basil, oregano and mint for the culinary desires of *Homo sapiens*, labiates are essential elements in any garden of earthly delights.

raising labiates FROM SEED

A number of the plants featured in this article seldom appear in the catalogs of even the best mail-order nurseries. Almost all, however, can be found in the annual seed-exchange lists published by organizations such as the Alpine Garden Society, the Hardy Plant Society, the North American Rock Garden Society, and the Scottish Rock Garden Club. Starting these plants from seed couldn't be easier. In January or February, sow the seeds thinly in a mix of equal parts soilless potting medium and coarse builder's sand. 4" pots are ideal for this purpose. Cover the seeds with about .125" of fine gravel (a bit coarser than the sand), then place the pots in the sink with 1" or so of water in it. When the gravel on top becomes darkened, the pots are saturated. Let the pots drain, then move them outdoors to a spot where they are somewhat protected and will not be subjected to winter sun, which can produce wide temperature fluctuations. Where winters are wet, some form of covering is advisable. When the weather begins to warm in spring, the seedlings will begin to germinate. Move them to a sunny or shady location, depending on their preference, and fertilize with a weak solution of all-purpose plant food every other week. Pot the seedlings up once they seem sturdy and have produced sets of true leaves.

Phlomis russeliana

Dracocephalum botryoides

LENTEN ROSE RENAISSANCE

recent breeding has brought fresh attention to this winter-blooming treasure

by THOMAS FISCHER

H. polyphylla var. chinensis

Although good-quality Lenten roses are much easier to find today than they were just a few years ago, they remain relatively expensive, and the best way to assemble an impressive collection of plants is to grow them yourself. A number of specialist nurseries offer seed by color, so if you're particularly interested in, say, light pink flowers, you can raise a whole batch. (It's a good idea to check whether the seed is hand-pollinated or open-pollinated; seedlings from hand-pollinated seed will bear a much higher percentage of flowers in the advertised color. On the other hand, open-pollinated seed can result in some interesting surprises.) If you decide to raise plants from seed, however, you'll need patience — the seeds can take up to six months or longer to germinate, and the plants themselves usually don't begin to bloom until their third year.

Seed should be sown as soon as you receive it — the earlier, the better. (The longer the seed is stored, the longer it will take to germinate.) Use any standard seedling or potting mixture. I've had good luck sowing about a dozen seeds per 4" plastic pot. Shallow flats will also give good results, but avoid using deep pots — the large volume of potting medium is not conducive to good germination. Space the seeds evenly, and cover them lightly with potting medium. If you like, you can top the pot off with about a .25" of grit, which is helpful in preventing damping off and the growth of algae or liverworts. Water each pot thoroughly.

You then have a choice: for quicker germination, keep the pots at about 70°F for three months, then place them in the refrigerator at 40°F for another three months. During the last month or so, check the pots frequently for signs of germination and remove any pot in which the seedlings have begun to sprout to a cool spot under strong fluorescent illumination (at least two 40-watt tubes) or a bright but not-too-sunny windowsill. The easier alternative is simply to place the pots in a protected corner outside and let nature take its course. The seedlings will appear in mid-spring once the weather has begun to warm. In either case, do not allow the potting mixture to dry out.

Once the seedlings have developed their first set of true leaves, pot them up individually and grow them on in a semishady spot for the summer. Feed them every other week with a balanced liquid fertilizer diluted according to the directions on the box. In early fall, plant the seedlings out in their permanent location. In all but the harshest climates, they shouldn't need winter protection. (Mulches have the unintended disadvantage of providing a haven for slugs.)

If you have a particularly prized specimen, you can increase it by division. The best time for this is summer, just as new root growth is beginning. Because of the plant's formidable root system, digging up a mature Lenten rose clump is no easy task — you'll need a stout gardening fork or two and perhaps an extra pair of hands as well. Don't dig too close to the stems — you want a generous root ball. Once the plant has been unearthed, shake any excess soil from the roots or wash the whole root ball off with a hose. Using a large, sturdy, sharp knife — and being extremely careful — cut the rootstock into divisions, each with two or three vigorous growing points and a set of roots. Replant the divisions in well-prepared soil and water them in thoroughly. When growth resumes, fertilize the division every month or so until the plant is well established. Lenten roses take a while to recover from division, so be patient.

Few perennials have been so relentlessly ballyhooed in recent years as the Lenten roses, the common name (for their habit of blooming in earliest spring) of a complex of hybrids known botanically as *Helleborus ×hybridus.* Usually I'm suspicious of ballyhoo of any sort, but in this case it's justified. Today's Lenten roses are the swans of the early-season garden, with long-lasting flowers in a huge range of subtle and sump-

A deep pink seedling raised by the author

A bed of mixed Lenten roses

tuous colors, thanks mainly to the intensive breeding and selection that have gone on in England, Germany and, more recently, in this country. Add that to handsome, almost evergreen foliage, and you get a plant that comes near to being a Platonic ideal among perennials.

The species that have given rise to these spectacular hybrids all belong to a closely related group whose native range stretches south and eastward from the Balkans into Greece and northern Turkey. One of the species, *H. orientalis,* from the area south and east of the Black Sea, is a vigorous plant with (depending on which subspecies you're looking at) creamy white flowers, or white flowers with crimson spots or reddish purple flowers. It has become so closely identified with the hybrid Lenten roses that they are often referred to as orientalis hybrids. While *H. orientalis* has certainly contributed its share of genes to the Lenten rose pool, it is hardly the only influence. The wide color range of the recent hybrids owes as much to the green-flowered *H. cyclophyllus* and *H. odorus,* the (sometimes) purple-black *H. torquatus,* and the highly variable *H. purpurascens,* among others.

Foliage Form and Color

So, what exactly has this potent genetic cocktail produced? Let's start with the foliage. Lenten roses have large (to 1.5' in diameter), leathery, dark green and slightly glossy leaves divided into (usually) seven to nine segments whose margins are serrate (that is, notched or toothed). The leaves are borne at the end of stalks that grow about 12" to 16" high, thus producing an umbrella-like effect. The clumps are strong-growing, and over time may get to be as much as a yard across. In milder parts of the country the foliage is evergreen, and even in areas near the

limits of the plant's hardiness (USDA Zone 5) will come through most of the winter in reasonably good shape. By late February, however, the wear and tear of the season starts to show, especially if snow cover has been lacking, and it's a good idea to cut the old foliage to the ground before the flower stalks begin to lengthen so that, later, you can enjoy the sight of flowers unencumbered by ratty leaves. When you undertake this task, be sure to wear gloves and a heavy, long-sleeved shirt. The edges of Lenten rose leaves are extremely sharp, and the plants themselves are highly poisonous. A short-sleeved foray into your Lenten rose patch can leave you with scores of fine scratches on your hands and arms, which in turn may cause you to feel ill for a few hours.

Flower Color

Dealing with old foliage will seem like a minor inconvenience, however, once you see the flowers. They are generally 2" to 3" across, with the showy part consisting of five rounded (or sometimes slightly pointed), overlapping sepals surrounding a cluster of small green nectaries (the true petals) and a boss of pale yellow stamens. Even ignoring its color, a Lenten rose flower looks shapely and well made, and may remind you of a single peony, which is no coincidence since both Lenten roses and peonies belong to the *Ranunculaceae,* the buttercup family.

But of course you can't ignore a Lenten rose's color, at least not for long. In one direction, the Lenten rose spectrum runs from sparkling white through ivory, cream, primrose, lemon and chartreuse to a vivid parrot green. In the other direction, white leads to palest pink and then, by countless fine degrees, to medium pink, rose, ruby, garnet, oxblood, amethyst, dusky purple, slate and finally to a voluptuous near-black. The darker shades are often accompanied by a light purple or bluish bloom, like that on a plum or a black grape, while the lighter colors can be solid or dappled with fine crimson or purple spots, which are sometimes so dense that they form solid patches. Interesting color blends also appear: primrose-yellow flowers may carry a flush of rose or crimson that from a slight distance reads as peach or apricot, and some breeders have concentrated on producing bicolors and picotees, or flowers in which the circle of nectaries is purple instead of green. My own favorite among the hundred-odd plants I grow has smoky lilac flowers with prominent, dark violet veins. Double Lenten roses also carry a great cachet among enthusiasts. Once extremely rare and expensive, they are becoming easier to find, although their quality varies — some are dull and messy-looking, while the best are exquisite, with clear colors and even rows of well-formed sepals.

Showing Off Your Hellebores

The flower's natural tendency is to be somewhat nodding, obliging you to lift it up if you want to examine its interior pattern. If this annoys you, look for plants with erect, outward-facing flowers — a trait that many breeders have been encouraging — or, if possible, plant your Lenten roses in a raised location.

The garden value of the flowers is greatly enhanced by their durability. You can count on a plant in bloom remaining attractive for six weeks or even longer, although the flowers will shed their nectaries and take on a greenish tinge after they have been pollinated (which can actually result in some interesting effects). Their bloom period varies with climate. In my Boston garden (Zone 6), they generally come into flower in mid-March with the earliest spring bulbs, and last well into May; in Atlanta and northern California I have seen clumps in full bloom in January. Eventually, the follicles — the maturing fruits — will swell with seeds, which they will disgorge in early summer. Lenten roses are prolific self-seeders, so if you do not want a swarm of youngsters crowding around the parent plant, you may want to remove the flowers before they shed their seed.

Lenten roses perform best in the conditions that their wild ancestors prefer: full to partial shade from deciduous trees; well-drained, humusy soil (think lots of leaf mold); and a reasonably steady supply of moisture, although a well-established clump can put up with a certain amount of dryness (and even competition from rooty trees like maples) thanks to its extensive and tenacious root system. If your plants start to wilt, you know it's time to give them a good, long, slow soaking. To keep the soil in my Lenten rose bed in good condition and to conserve moisture, I put down a 2" layer of shredded oak leaves each fall.

Special Care

Many garden writers have commented on how greedy Lenten roses are, and how they have to be showered with wheelbarrow-loads of well-rotted manure. I find that my layer of mulch, plus an annual sprinkling of balanced, slow-release fertilizer applied just as the flower stalks begin to lengthen, works just fine. After all, we're not talking about giant pumpkins.

Lenten roses are subject to few ills, although gardeners who live in damp, mild-winter areas may experience occasional black spotting and streaking of the flowers caused by various fungi. If you use fungicides, you may want to take action; my inclination would be to let things alone and hope for drier weather next year. The one pest I find regularly troublesome is the aphid, or rather, the aphid and her large extended family, for when they show up, it seems to be by the millions. Insecticidal soap makes quick work of them.

Landscaping Uses

Assuming that your garden offers the conditions that Lenten roses need to thrive, what should you do with them? First of all, with their dense leafage, they make a superb groundcover for shade, and the flower colors, whether dark or pale, all harmonize nicely. If you only have room for a few specimens, plant them where you can get a good close look at the flowers — a shady edge of the terrace, perhaps. You're not going to want to go traipsing off to the back 40 to admire the hellebores when it's 36°F and threatening sleet. Although some books go into great detail about suitable planting companions, there's no point in getting too fussy. Basically, you want companions that, like the Lenten roses themselves, bloom early and like shade. Snowdrops look splendid with Lenten roses of any color (but especially with the blacks and purples), and should be planted in as large a quantity as your pocketbook will permit. Blue-flowered pulmonarias nicely complement the reds and pinks, while pink-flowered pulmonarias are lovely with white Lenten roses, as are bright gold winter aconites. As a frontal plant, consider the low-growing, shade-loving, evergreen perennial *Cardamine trifolia*, with small, white flowers that may remind you of iberis. One last suggestion: If you can, plant your deep red Lenten roses where the low winter sun can shine through their sepals. No stained glass in any cathedral in the world is more glorious.

THE ALLURE OF BLUE POPPIES

success with meconopsis is the crowning achievement of any gardener

by GRAHAM STUART THOMAS

Meconopsis betonicifolia

The genus *Meconopsis* has an unusual distinction among hardy plants in that the different species embrace all three primary colors — true blue, red and yellow. I can think of only a few other genera of similar colors, *Gentiana*, *Delphinium* and *Salvia* among them. Apart from other characters, the species of *Meconopsis* differ from those of *Papaver*, the true poppies, in the shape of their seed capsules. In *Papaver* they are covered with a sort of disk or lid, whereas in *Meconopsis* (which means "poppylike") they open longitudinally. Apart from one species, all meconopsis are natives of the eastern Himalayas and western China. The exception is *M. cambrica*, which is a native of western Europe and Britain, and is known as the Welsh poppy. It may be vivid lemon yellow, soft orange or even scarlet, but I have yet to see a merging of the various tints. They are sound perennials, thriving under shady trees, and they are reliable spreaders by seed. Double forms of each color are known but, though they may occur from seed, they are best increased by careful division in early spring.

The other perennial species have a long history, several having been in cultivation for well over 100 years, and yet in spite of their beauty they remain comparatively uncommon. To start with, they are plants that thrive only in cool woodland conditions, on lime-free soil with plenty of humus. Such is their beauty when growing well that a poor specimen is not worth a second glance. The magic is, of course, in having blue poppies. We are used to flaming reds in the Oriental poppies and various exquisite tints in the Shirley and Iceland poppies, but to *Meconopsis* is reserved that rare color, true blue.

As long ago as 1848, M. *simplicifolia* was introduced from Nepal and Tibet but, in spite of its color, violet or blue, it has remained rare and difficult to cultivate. The so-called lampshade poppy, *M. integrifolia,* is a hairy plant with clear yellow nodding flowers but it is not reliably perennial; the other well-known yellow species, *M. villosa,* is and has been grown under this name (or as *Cathcartia villosa*) since 1851. The so-called harebell poppy, *M. quintuplinervia*, a term coined by Reginald Farrer, has proved a true perennial since 1877. It makes a tuft of leaves above which hang on 1'-high stalks, bells of pale lavender with dark violet blotches around the cream stamens. It is a plant of great beauty.

growing meconopsis IN THE UNITED STATES

Few perennials inspire such immediate adoration as the Himalayan blue poppies, but the painful truth is that they are growable only within strict climatic limits. Winter cold is not the problem — many species thrive in Alaska, which makes them hardy to at least USDA Zone 3 or 4. Their true enemies are dryness and especially heat. They must be planted in acidic, humus-rich soil that never, repeat never, dries out entirely, and if summer temperatures, particularly at night, climb much above the low 80s for extended periods, they will go into a decline and eventually die. In practical terms, this means that, in the continental United States, they can be expected to thrive only along the Pacific Coast from the Bay Area northward; along the Maine coast; inland at higher elevations elsewhere in New England; and perhaps in northern New York and Michigan's Upper Peninsula. (*Meconopsis cambrica* and some of the blue-flowered annual species such as *M. horridula* are a bit more forgiving.) By taking heroic measures to create cool, moist microclimates, gardeners in areas as hot and dry as Southern California have been able to get blue poppies to survive, but unless you are of a quixotic (not to say masochistic) temperament, it is best to admire these beauties from afar if your conditions are not conducive to their survival.

Meconopsis grandis

Meconopsis ×sheldonii

Meconopsis cambrica

In 1904, two outstanding species were introduced to British gardens: the true red *M. punicea*, with nodding flowers on single stems after the style of *M. quintuplinervia*, and the dainty, tall, branching *M. chelidoniifolia*. This is another good perennial, achieving some 5' in good conditions, every shoot ending with a nodding small bloom of clear lemon yellow. It is easy to increase from division, like the harebell poppy. *Meconopsis punicea* died out in Britain but was reintroduced.

All of the above have undoubted charm but are apt to take a back seat when we consider the heavyweights of the genus — *M. grandis* (1895) and *M. betonicifolia* of 1924, at which time it was known as *M. baileyi*. Because of cross-pollination, these and their hybrid, *M. ×sheldonii*, have become rather confused in gardens, but I will try to sort them out.

Although *M. grandis* has been known since 1895, it did not become generally grown until later introductions brought it to the fore. There are some superlative things among them. George Sherriff; Stainton, Sykes and Williams; and later Ludlow and Sherriff all introduced stunning forms of gorgeous true blue, upstanding and regal and having the easily recognized character of producing their stout flowering stalks from one point on a common central stem, well above the hairy, toothed, basal leaves. They all hail from western China, Sikkim, and other Himalayan countries and, provided they are lifted and divided every few years and given fresh supplies of humus, will usually prove true perennials. Some are inclined to be purplish but a true blue causes a gasp of astonishment from the beholder. The *grandis* strain GS 600 (also known as 'Sherriff No. 600') is one of the most magnificent forms. They were all brought from the wild in the third quarter of the 20th century.

Meanwhile, in 1924 *M. betonicifolia* burst upon the gardening public. It was then known erroneously as *M. baileyi*, and I was lucky enough to flower it in my father's garden, thanks to the generosity of a friend, in 1927. Having been written about freely by its discoverer, Frank Kingdon-Ward, it was a great triumph, I can assure you, to have "the blue poppy" in our little patch. It is quite different from *M. grandis*. Reaching to 4' or more, the topmost leading bud opens first, followed by subsequent buds borne in the axils of the leafy erect stem, well above the basal leaves, lobed or toothed like those of a betony. It flowers rather later than *M. grandis* and has flowers somewhat smaller and of a paler blue, but with the same dark yellow stamens. While it can be regarded as a true perennial, it is best not to let young plants flower before they have produced a second rosette of leaves and, to keep the plants in good health, they need division every few years, as for *M. grandis*, with plenty of additional humus. Opinions differ as to the best time for division; on the whole I prefer mid- or late September to the spring.

It was inevitable that with seed raising as the most popular method of increase, hybrids should occur between these two noble species. But the first deliberate cross was made in Surrey, England in 1937 by a Mr. Sheldon, and is therefore known as *M. ×sheldonii*. Of all the blue poppies, it is the most vigorous and heat resistant. The same cross was made later in Scotland, and a resulting plant was handed down between friends until it reached Leslie Slinger of the famous Slieve Donard Nursery in Northern Ireland. Slinger at once recognized the value of this freely increasing plant, and having no name for it decided to call it 'Slieve Donard'. As such it has become very famous, with flowers of a clear and vivid blue with dark yellow stamens. It is otherwise midway between these two species. Its long flowering stalks lead one to think automatically of *M. grandis*.

Another very vigorous and famous plant is known as 'Branklyn'. Although originally thought to be a form of *M. grandis* GS 600, I feel sure that it should be included under *M. ×sheldonii*. It is bursting with vigor, but like the others needs regular renewal of soil and division, and its blue is tainted with purple. There is no doubt that had it not been for the pure blues among these species, those of rich purple, such as 'Keillour Purple', and perhaps also some of the lilac forms of *M. betonicifolia*, would have had many admirers. There is a beautiful lemon-white hybrid called *M. ×sarsonsii* (*M. betonicifolia* × *M. integrifolia*) worth looking out for.

All meconopsis flower in the magic month of June, and make a lovely contrast with cool-tinted azaleas and primulas, which fortunately enjoy the same conditions. They grow best where the sun is filtered by a light canopy of tree branches, or in the shade from a high wall, and are never so good as when the air is cool and charged with moisture.

Meconopsis betonicifolia, lilac form

PARIS IN THE SPRING

Asia, not Europe, is the center of these elegant woodland perennials

by DANIEL J. HINKLEY

The genus *Paris* comprises a group of woodland perennials with an elegant and understated allure that stirs the blood of serious gardeners.

Although the name of the genus is identical to that of the French city, they have different origins, the plant genus having been named for its equal numbers of floral parts and leaves (from the Latin *par* or *paris*, meaning equal), whereas the city received its name from the Parisii, an ancient Celtic tribe. Closely allied to the genus *Trillium* and assigned to the family Trilliaceae, *Paris* occurs only in the Old World, and is geographically centered in China, with 23 of the 26 known species occurring within its borders, and 12 species endemic to that country. Only two species occur in Europe.

Though there are significant differences between the species, all exhibit an arrangement of foliage and flower that makes virtually any member of the genus recognizable. The single flowers are borne slightly above a whorl of four to ten leaves on stems from 6" to 6' from early to late spring. The flowers are composed of broad green (occasionally white) outer tepals and (in most species) threadlike, golden inner tepals. Yellow anthers surround a globular pistil of green, violet or (rarely) white.

The European Species

Paris quadrifolia is the type species, usually more highly esteemed in homoeopathic medicine than in the garden. It is common in cool, moist woods throughout most of northern Europe, Siberia and northern China, where it has garnered such vernacular names as true love, one berry, wolf berry and herb paris. The four (or occasionally five) broadly ovate leaves of the species are borne atop stems to 6", capped by diminutive flowers of green outer tepals and wispy greenish white inner tepals in May and June. Pollination is effected by flies attracted by a reportedly disagreeable smell, and is followed by striking, plump, dull blue berries.

The other European representative of the genus occurs further to the east, where I have observed it in the Pontic Alps of northeastern Turkey. There, *P. incompleta* grows at rather high elevations, always in association with the Oriental beech, *Fagus orientalis*. Whorls of five to nine narrow leaves are carried atop stems to 1', while the flowers rising slightly above, as its specific epithet implies, lack the whorl of inner tepals. The fruit is a simple berry of glistening purple black.

Paris In Japan and Korea

A total of three species of *Paris* occur in these countries, two of which are quite similar to their European counterparts. *Paris tetraphylla* is common in the moist, cool mountains of northern Honshu and Hokkaido, where it can be found growing beneath dense stands of cercidiphyllums and magnolias in thickets of *Aucuba japonica, Skimmia japonica, Pachysandra terminalis* and *Trillium tschonoskii*. As its specific epithet implies, this species normally possesses four broad leaves atop stems to 10", while the broad outer tepals become strongly reflexed

Paris polyphylla var. *chinesis*

Perhaps because of their scarceness in cultivation, paris have garnered an undeserved reputation for being difficult and resentful of disturbance and division. In the cool, moist climate of the Pacific Northwest, the genus presents few challenges. I cultivate a large collection of *Paris* species in well-drained, humus-rich, slightly acidic soil under a high overstory of Douglas firs, and similar woodland conditions would seem the best bet in other parts of the country. However, I have also encountered thriving specimens sited in full sun and growing in clay soils in southeastern England.

Plants can be propagated by seed or division, though the latter is much easier. (Like trillium seeds, the seed of paris possesses a double dormancy, and may take up to three years to germinate, with an additional three to five years to first blossoming.) A plant that is dug up in early spring as vegetative growth resumes will reveal an abundance of dormant buds along the rhizome. If a piece of the rhizome with one or more of these buds is removed and replanted, it will usually break growth the same spring, although some divisions may remain dormant for an additional year. Root growth begins in late summer and early autumn, and it is best to avoid disturbing the plants during that time.

1. *Paris rugosa* **2.** *Paris polyphylla* var. *chinensis* **3.** *Paris polyphylla* var. *yunnanensis* **4.** *Paris thibetica* **5.** *Paris polyphylla* var. *stenophylla* **6.** *Paris polyphylla* var. *polyphylla*

Paris polyphylla var. chinensis

TYPE OF PLANT: herbaceous perennials **FAMILY:** Trilliaceae (trillium family), formerly Liliaceae **ORIGINS:** temperate Europe to eastern Asia **HARDINESS:** USDA Zones 5/6–9 (most species) **HEIGHT:** 6"–6', depending on species **LEAVES:** borne in an apical whorl of 4–10, obovate to linear, acuminate, to 12" long, medium green, sometimes variegated **FLOWERS:** spidery, with 4–8 (usually) broad, green outer tepals and 4–8 (usually) narrow, yellow inner tepals and up to 20 stamens **FRUIT:** a simple berry or a fleshy capsule containing (usually) scarlet seeds **BLOOM PERIOD:** early–late spring **SOIL:** humusy, moisture retentive, well drained **EXPOSURE:** dappled shade **WATERING:** not tolerant of drought **PLANTING TIME:** spring; do not move plants in summer and fall **FEEDING:** annual mulch of leaf mold (optional) **PROPAGATION:** by division in spring or ripe seed sown in fall **PROBLEMS:** none serious

facts and FIGURES

shortly after opening. Upon ripening, the plump, blue-black berry is sometimes accentuated by the outer tepals taking on hues of violet.

Growing at lower elevations, often in valley bottoms, throughout much of Japan, Korea and China, is *P. verticillata*, which bears false terminal whorls of five to eight narrowly oblong, short-petioled leaves to 6" atop 8" to 16" stems. Both the outer green tepals and golden inner tepals become strongly reflexed upon fertilization, which results in a small black fruit. Like *P. quadrifolia* and *P. tetraphylla*, this species has formed sizable stoloniferous colonies in our woodland garden. To my knowledge, this species offers the only double-flowered form of any paris. With a trebling of the outer tepals, *P. verticillata* 'Flore Pleno' presents a beguiling display of precious green "roses," though it is rarely available, and then only for a princely sum.

Paris japonica is certainly the most distinctive of the genus as well as the most challenging to grow. Above false whorls of six to eight broadly ovate leaves appear striking flowers composed of linear white outer tepals and narrow bright golden inner tepals. *Paris japonica* is found only in the moist, subalpine meadows of the Japanese Archipelago, where it occurs in great abundance. Because of its exacting climatic and soil requirements, most of the specimens purchased worldwide probably fail to establish.

China's Riches

Current taxonomy suggests that six additional taxa within the subgenus *Paris* occur within China. I suspect that few of these, however, are in commerce under valid names. With that said, I have successfully germinated and brought to flower *P. rugosa*, a beautiful species from Sichuan Province that possesses four glossy green, somewhat undulated leaves on short stems to 5". The flowers, of four green outer sepals and golden strands of inner sepals, result in a large, single, succulent red berry.

If the nomenclature of the subgenus *Paris* is in trouble, the taxonomy of the subgenus *Daiswa* is in international crisis. Enter *P. polyphylla*. This widely distributed and notoriously variable species has undoubtedly been in cultivation longer than any other paris. Ornamentally speaking, it is truly sensational, though I hesitate to define what actually comprises this taxa. I have encountered vast colonies of the typical Himalayan form of this species, *P. polyphylla* var. *polyphylla*, in eastern Nepal growing at relatively low elevations in moist, shaded forests. This form produces a whorl of seven to ten dark green linear leaves held by long purple petioles atop stems to 12". On short pedicels above the foliage, the typical paris flowers of broad green outer tepals and wiry golden inner tepals surround (after fertilization) a swollen, green, berrylike capsule that splits and expands to reveal a treasure trove of brilliant scarlet (occasionally yellow) seeds. It is my experience that the Himalayan populations of this species emerge much earlier in the spring than the Chinese varieties, and are in full blossom by early May in our USDA Zone 8, maritime climate.

The first paris that I grew under the name of *P. polyphylla*, however, is an utterly different creature. Often not appearing aboveground until mid-June, the leaves and flowers unfurl like scepters of fine art glass as the stems rise to 4' or more. Ovate leaves ultimately expand to 10" in length, while the typical flowers of green and gold remain unblemished for a full four months. I credit this characteristic to the lack of a compatible partner for cross-pollination and hence fertilization, as I have never had seed produced on this clone.

Other Asian Species

The tallest of all paris I have encountered is *P. vietnamensis*, from the mountainous region of Fan Xi Phan in northern Vietnam. Here the plants rose to an astounding 6' or more, with substantive whorls of leaves to 1' and large disks of green-tepaled flowers. As it is from relatively low elevations, it is unlikely to prove hardy in temperate climates, though it will certainly make for an enticing candidate for containerization, a method of cultivation to which the genus as a whole seems very adaptable.

Two species in subgenus *Daiswa* are known for their colorfully veined leaves, intricately netted in silvers and yellows. *Paris luquanensis* has proven to be extremely gardenworthy, with squat stems to 4" carrying four rounded ovate leaves that appear almost cyclamenlike. The demure flowers, held slightly above this handsome foliage, curiously lower themselves to ground level after fertilization, while offering a startling display of orange-red fruit in late autumn. The foliage of *P. marmorata* differs primarily in possessing a leaf undersurface of purple red and outer tepals veined in silver white.

Certainly the years ahead will give us a better understanding of the taxonomy and natural distribution of this remarkable genus. Fortunately, we don't need to wait until then to appreciate its remarkable qualities in our gardens. The genus *Paris* awaits a wider audience that will soon enough, and for good reasons, be singing its praises.

PENSTEMON: THE ALL-AMERICAN PERENNIAL

these tough, colorful natives take dryness and poor soil in stride

by LAUREN SPRINGER

Rare is the gardener who never falls prey to a plant obsession. What to do when the object of desire is an entire genus, and one that comprises more than 250 species?

The affair becomes intense and long-term, with enough fascination, frustration and fulfillment to last a lifetime. Such is the case for those of us smitten by the *Penstemon* clan, that alluring genus of North and Central American perennials and subshrubs. We call ourselves penstemaniacs.

The genus *Penstemon* belongs to the *Scrophulariaceae*, a family noted for the showy flowers of members such as foxgloves, veronicas and snapdragons. Most species grow wild in sunny, harsh regions of the western half of the continent; the epicenter is Utah, boasting more than 70 indigenous species. Like the colorful historical characters who populate the lore of the West, many of these flamboyant plants resent civilization, often proving maddeningly difficult to tame in the garden. I killed one particular species year after year, while just half a mile away on a clay escarpment it mocked my gardening attempts with great blue sheets of bloom each spring. Yet not all penstemons play hard to get. There are enough adaptable species to satisfy all but the most ravenous penstemaniac. These amenable, relatively tall evergreen plants are the focus here; they are more useful in most garden settings and styles than the low-growing, often persnickety rock-garden types and offer the beauty of the European hybrids with the hardiness and vigor necessary in much of North America.

These tractable penstemons come in a color range few other genera can boast. There are pastels — soft lavenders, pinks, whites and pale yellows. And there are the exciting, richly saturated blues, purples, crimsons and orange reds. The flowers arrange themselves either in clusters or singly along strongly upright stems. These flashy spikes lend a much-needed contrast to the predominantly rounded, mounded look of so many garden perennials.

Adaptable Penstemons

One of the best places to see a great number of the taller, showier *Penstemon* species is at the Horticultural Research Center of the University of Nebraska in North Platte, where entire fields are given up to their testing and hybridization. In mid-June the place is overcome by penstemonium — row upon row of plants that have the flash to match the most sumptuous garden perennial yet still retain the airy, untamed grace of a wildflower. The Research Center is also home of the famed *P. digitalis* selection 'Husker Red', so named for its unusual red-tinted foliage, a hue it shares with the university's popular football team, the Cornhuskers. The white, early-summer flowers, rising to 3', have an ever-so-slight blush of pink and make good cut subjects as well.

Penstemon barbatus

Unfortunately, in the mad fervor this plant created when it debuted, many nurseries began propagating it by seed rather than vegetatively, and the distinctive foliage color was lost in much of the material available. *Penstemon digitalis*, one of the longest-lived of the genus, has an easterly natural distribution and performs better than most in regions with heavy rainfall and wet winters. It also boasts attractive, shiny, maroon seedpods. Closely related, slightly shorter *P. gracilis* and *P. hirsutus* have cool, lavender-gray flowers and are also good choices for humid climates. Rose-purple cousin *P. smallii* is perhaps the best penstemon for the South, where in a most unpenstemonial manner it thrives in damp, even shaded sites.

Big, Showy Flowers

Just northwest of North Platte, in the soft, undulating country known as the Sandhills, another easy-to-please penstemon can be found growing wild. Rising above feathery June grass, blue spiderwort and golden puccoon are the stately lavender, pink or rarely white spikes of *P. grandiflorus*, known in the nursery trade as shell-leaf penstemon. Some Great Plains folk have a better name for it — wild snapdragon

All of the easy-to-please *Penstemon* species have a wide range of hardiness — from USDA Zone 3 or 4 to Zone 8 or 9 — accustomed as they are to the extremes of a continental climate with its intense summer heat and sunlight and brutal, often snowless winter cold. The one requirement they share is good drainage, especially during their dormant season. In areas with wet winters, planting on a slope or in raised beds helps, and heavy soils should be amended with sand and grit. Many penstemons actually delight in clay soil, but only in semiarid regions where waterlogging is not an issue. High pH doesn't bother them, either. In too rich a soil, however, they live a short life in the fast lane, growing swollen and falling over like debauchees and then often succumbing to the first rigors of winter.

Penstemon digitalis 'Husker Red' in a border setting

— which captures the essence of the huge, 2", snout-shaped, waxy blossoms. This is truly one of North America's most spectacular wildflowers, and not in the least bit fussy. It grows wild from Texas up to the Canadian border, in sand and clay, in established grassland and disturbed field. Abundant water in spring and summer only makes for larger, fatter plants. Dale Lindgren, professor at the North Platte campus of the University of Nebraska, has selected seed strains for color: 'Prairie Snow' is dependably pure white, while 'War Axe' features deep pinks and purples. *Penstemon grandiflorus* does not bloom for long — two weeks in late spring is typical — but the rounded, blue, eucalyptus-like foliage has year-long appeal. Like the rest of the genus, it sets copious seed and lives longer and more vigorously if only a small percentage is allowed to ripen. Penstemons wear themselves out with their prodigious progeny; leaving one flowering stalk per group of plants should provide all the insurance seed necessary.

Only two other penstemons come close to *P. grandiflorus* in flower size. Southern native *P. cobaea* is usually white, but rose-flowered forms also exist. It has a bulky, green rosette of foliage and can take heat and humidity as well as a bit of shade, but is not as free-flowering as some of the other adaptable species. *Penstemon palmeri* is a southwestern native that has proven hardy in Zone 4. A giant in the genus, it can reach 6' in bloom, with great wands of blush pink, fragrant, bulbous blossoms in the summer. My daughter thinks the gaping flowers look like fat, laughing fish. The serrated, turquoise-blue foliage is equally striking. This plant insists on very dry conditions in winter.

I find another southwestern species, *P. clutei*, easier to accommodate in the garden. Although it also prefers dry sites, it tolerates the spring muck that melting snow makes of my heavy clay and goes on to bloom vibrantly in early summer, albeit at half the height of *P. palmeri*. The bright pink flowers have amber overtones that give it the common name sunset penstemon, and the foliage is also a bright turquoise. Often the difference between life and death by water has to do not with how much but with when. Many of the early bloomers tend to tolerate more late-winter and spring moisture, while many of the mid- and late-summer bloomers like a dry winter and spring, with summer water similar to the monsoonal rain patterns of their native haunts.

intriguing FLOWER SHAPES

Penstemons are also known as beardtongues for the often hairy, sterile fifth stamen that lolls in the mouth of the flower. All penstemon flowers share a characteristic shape: five petals fuse to form a tube that then separates and flares at the opening, two petal lobes at the top and three at the bottom. Some species have plumper, more widely opened flowers to accommodate bees and bumblebees, often in a most droll manner when the insect becomes briefly entrapped and sends the whole flower stalk into violent vibrations. Other species have longer, narrower flowers — in bright red, orange and rose pink — that allow entry to only the thin, probing beak of a hummingbird.

Penstemon strictus (front)

Tough Ones

A penstemon for cool, consistently moist conditions is indigo-blue *P. rydbergii*, with small but brilliant flowers in phlomis-like whorls on 2' stalks. Similarly hued but much coarser and showier is the 2' to 3' Rocky Mountain penstemon, *P. strictus*, and its floriferous selection 'Bandera'. This species is quite tolerant of spring and early-summer moisture but resents high humidity, as do its close cousins the truer, lighter blue Great Plains native *P. glaber* and finer-textured, slightly shorter Wasatch Mountains native *P. cyananthus*. All three have glossy, emerald-green foliage in dense, ground-hugging rosettes.

For climates with hot summers and warm nights, the *P. barbatus* selections and hybrids are best. Long-blooming, 4' to 6' *P. barbatus*, the southwestern scarlet bugler, with its characteristic tubular, shark's-head-shaped flowers, is usually bright scarlet but ranges into pink, peach, yellow and even white. It can tolerate moisture but flops on its side unless grown lean and mean. Not so the 12" to 15" 'Elfin Pink', a superb, vigorous cultivar with bright pink flowers. Seed strains derived from the scarlet bugler, all shorter and including pink, crimson, pure red and purple individuals, include var. *praecox* f. *nanus*, also known as 'Rondo'; 'Scharf Hybrids'; and 'Saskatoon Hybrids'. The purple hues no doubt are due to the influx of some blue-flowered species. Again, Dale Lindgren of Nebraska is to thank for some excellent plants, in this case *P. barbatus* hybrids with 'Prairie' in their names. 'Prairie Fire' is a bright red, compact grower; 'Prairie Dawn' a good pink; and 'Prairie Dusk' a rich purple, much praised by frustrated penstemon-smitten gardeners in the Middle Atlantic and southern states.

For early and late reds in the garden, spring-blooming firecracker penstemon, *P. eatonii*, and subshrubby, late-summer-flowering *P. rostriflorus* help lengthen the season of adaptable penstemons. Hummingbirds much appreciate the extended months of available nectar. Both are hardy into Zone 4, with the latter sometimes suffering some dieback but recovering vigorously from the base.

Looking Ahead

Another person who figures importantly in the penstemon hybridizing world is Bruce Meyers from Washington State. His 'Mexicali Hybrids' have the large flowers, jewel tones, and often contrasting throat colors and markings so appealing in the tender European hybrids, but on much hardier, more compact plants. Subshrubby and well clothed in pointed, narrow, light green foliage, these plants flower for more than two months, from midsummer well into autumn — no mean feat for a penstemon. They come true from seed. In Colorado, two selections were made for exceptional hardiness and floral performance: vibrant 'Red Rocks' and 'Pikes Peak Purple'. They are being propagated by cuttings for national distribution through the Plant Select program coordinated by the Denver Botanic Gardens and Colorado State University. Top honors for long bloom, however, are reserved for a Pacific Northwest native. *Penstemon richardsonii*, a subshrub with profuse, blue-gray, hollylike serrated foliage, sends up lipstick-pink flowers for four months. It takes light shade in regions with hot summers or intense sunlight; indeed, it is a dry shade plant of choice in my garden.

And now, what to do with all these gardenworthy penstemons? Few plants have their stylistic versatility. They blended as effortlessly into the traditional dry flower borders and effusive cottage look of my former garden as they do in my present naturalistic garden, threading through grasses and mingling with lichen-covered boulders. The truth is, once penstemania hits, no well drained place is safe from the seductive charms of these wonderful, all-American plants.

growing penstemons FROM SEED

Many penstemons are not available in the nursery trade, or only in very localized areas such as Denver and Santa Fe. Fortunately, this group of plants is one of the easiest to grow from seed. Penstemon seed has a long shelf life — I've had success with 10-year-old leftovers. In fact, many of the prairie species need a period of dry storage before they germinate. Species from mountainous regions tend to have a cold-stratification requirement, while many of the desert species do not. I sow all mine in early winter in a sterile, gritty medium and put the pots outside in a dependably cold, shaded place for the rest of the season; stratification doesn't harm those that don't need it. Keep excess rain off the pots — ideally, they should get buried in snow. In April, the narrow cotyledons of the seedlings begin to emerge and the pots are quickly given a place in the sun. Most young penstemons respond well to feeding — I nourish the seedlings with a one-quarter-strength fertilizer solution each time I water them. They are transplanted to individual pots in June, and are usually fat and sassy enough to go in the garden by late summer or fall.

A PARADE OF POPPIES

flamboyant and easy to grow, these charmers thrive on neglect and poor soil

by LAUREN SPRINGER

They appear on Ukrainian easter eggs, preserved in ancient Egyptian tombs and in John McCrae's famous poem, "In Flanders Fields," as symbols of the bloodshed of war.

Across many cultures, poppies have more than their share of passionate devotees. And no wonder; the showy, simple yet sensual blossom of a poppy speaks the essence of flower. Fortunately, those smitten by poppies are in luck — there are more than 70 species of so-called true poppies (the genus *Papaver*) alone, and 22 more genera with some 250 species in the family Papaveraceae. What's more, most are garden-worthy. Best of all, a passion for poppies brings fast, inexpensive results — the majority grow easily from seed.

All but a handful of poppies hark from the temperate regions of the northern hemisphere. Most are herbaceous plants — annuals, perennials and a few biennials. Their characteristic yellow, white or orange sap contains bitter, often poisonous alkaloids, which probably accounts for their general freedom from pests, both insect and mammalian. Aside from slugs, which occasionally enjoy the foliage of the woodland species (a distinct group not treated here), seemingly the only creature tempted by poppies is *Homo sapiens*, be it for the vase, garden, strudel or opium den.

The sun-loving poppy genera come in every flower color but blue. With the exception of the petalless plume poppies, the blossoms are rounded in outline, either flat or cupped, and often have prominent stamens. Individual poppy blossoms tend to be fleeting, yet many species send up an exuberant number of buds over a long period of time. The fruits that follow can also be ornamental. The ample capsules, whether elongated or plump and barrel-like, are perfectly suited for dispersing copious quantities of small, rounded seeds.

Hunnemannia fumariifolia

Papaver sendtneri

Among the most delightful and tractable poppies are the abundantly self-sowing annual species. These should be sown directly into the garden in fall or early spring; their brittle taproots do not take kindly to transplanting. Once sown, they reappear year after year, adding wonderful spontaneity with their unexpected, cheerful faces. These annuals are also among the most adaptable poppies, thriving in almost any soil except a poorly drained one. In hot regions, they bloom in winter and early spring; in temperate climes, late spring and early summer; where summers are cool, their display continues through August.

Perhaps the most evocative of the annual species are the red poppies that spangle open, cultivated lands throughout Europe and much of Asia. Comprising eight or nine species, these common yet beautiful wildflowers have enchanted people for millennia. The most commonly available of the annual red poppies is *Papaver rhoeas*, the corn poppy, a branched, bristly-stemmed, 1' to 3' plant with 3" flowers. The best-known strain, the Shirley poppies, were named for a 19th-century vicar of Shirley who selected red, lavender and rose picotee, or white-edged forms from wild poppy populations in Surrey, England. Among the strains currently available, 'Angel's Choir' features flouncy double-flowered forms in soft, feminine colors. Perhaps the most sought-after strain of corn poppy is 'Mother of Pearl', selected by British garden sophisticate Sir Cedric Morris. The flowers come in haunting shades of smoky lavender, peach, mauve, white and opalescent gray — perfect for gardens where red is not welcome.

For drier, hotter gardens, the Mediterranean and central Asian annual red poppies are a better bet. These are altogether more diminutive and wilder-looking than the corn poppy, and include *Roemeria refracta*, *Papaver arenarium*, *P. dubium*, *P. pavoninum* and *P. commutatum*. Unlike its kindred, *P. commutatum* has distinctive black blotches in the middle of each petal rather than at the base, hence its cultivar name 'Lady Bird'. These species can be tricky to locate, but most appear now and again in seed exchanges. (Another member of this group, the beautiful opium poppy, *P. somniferum*, has been the target of a DEA crackdown; it is legal to sell and possess seeds of the plant, but not to grow it.)

From the dry regions of the Americas comes another lovely group of poppies. Some are true annuals; others are perennial in their native habitats yet grow well as self-sowing annuals elsewhere. They make exceptional garden plants by virtue of their extended bloom period and attractive foliage. The 10 or so species of the genus *Eschscholzia* are all characterized by ferny foliage, a caplike calyx that pops off dramatically as the flowers open, and long, narrow fruit capsules. These sun worshipers close their flowers into narrow tubes at night and on cloudy days. The California poppy (*E. californica*), an 8" to 18" short-lived perennial, is typically golden orange. White, cream, pale yellow, rose, crimson, scarlet and two-toned selections exist, as do semidoubles ('Mission Bells', 'Dali', 'Rose Chiffon' and 'Jersey Cream') and those with fringed or fluted petals ('Ballerina', 'Apricot Flambeau', 'Thai Silk' and 'Sugared Almonds'). And yet if there is but one orange flower to let loose in one's garden, let it be the California poppy: the bright, silken petals set against the finely cut blue foliage represents a perfect marriage of leaf and flower. Two dainty, 6" annual species, both with yellow flowers above gray-green leaves, are also sometimes offered: *E. lobbii* and *E. caespitosa*. The latter comes in a fragrant, pale yellow form called 'Sundew'. Neither of these flower as long as *E. californica*, which blooms for months on end until extreme heat, hard frost or soggy winters put an end to it.

Mexican tulip poppy (*Hunnemannia fumariifolia*) looks for all intents and purposes like a taller, larger form of the California

Papaver orientale 'Patty's Plum'

poppy. Perennial in mild, dry climates and annual elsewhere, its 3" golden goblets bloom for months, beautiful with blue flax. They make excellent cut flowers as well, with a perplexingly elusive fragrance.

The showiest of the New World genera is *Argemone*, the prickly poppies. It's beyond me why these aren't found in more gardens. They certainly aren't picky about culture; I sent seed of a Colorado foothills native to a friend in Ireland who has grown it in a scree bed for several years now. Like cacti, these poppies combine sumptuous yet delicate blossoms with stiff, wickedly thorny stems and leaves.

Argemone polyanthemos

Prickly poppy foliage is lobed, gray green or bluish, and often with prominent white veination; the flowers range from 2" to 6" in diameter. Of the tender species that do well as annuals, *A. mexicana* 'Yellow Lustre' and the paler *A. ochroleuca* have flashy yellow flowers; *A. grandiflora*, *A. munita* and *A. platyceras* bloom white. The hardier, short-lived perennial prickly poppies from the United States are all white flowered. These make excellent, quick-growing yet well-behaved substitutes for the glorious but invasive tree poppy, *Romneya coulteri*, which only large, warm, West Coast gardens can host. Invite any of the following species into the garden: *A. hispida*, *A. squarrosa* or *A. polyanthemos*, commonly known as cowboy's fried egg, whose satiny flowers shimmer along the road to our house.

Mountain Poppies

In regions where summers don't get infernally hot, poppies that naturally occur at high altitudes will thrive and self-sow. These short-lived perennials are tough, taking frigid winters and requiring little moisture or nourishment. Their seemingly fragile petals hold up remarkably well; in our Colorado foothills gusts I watch bees and bumblebees hang on for the ride as the poppies bob up and down. Most of these plants are diminutive, forming a basal rosette of foliage from which a long succession of solitary 1" to 2" yellow, orange, peach, pink or white flowers arise on leafless stems rarely more than 1' in height.

The name *Papaver alpinum* is actually a collective name for a number of similar European species. These plants are most popular among rock gardeners but make lovely subjects for a naturalistic garden, especially on a hillside or in gravel where they consort beautifully with small species of tufted grasses and sedges. *Papaver sendtneri* and *P. burseri* (sometimes seen as *P. alpinum* 'Album') are white; *P. kerneri* and *P. rhaeticum* are yellow. These alpine poppies have arctic and Asian counterparts: luminescent pale yellow *P. miyabeanum* and *P. fauriei* from Japan; nodding white or pale pink *P. alboroseum*; golden *P. nivale*; and yellow, pink or white *P. radicatum*, the true Iceland poppy.

The plants commonly known as Iceland poppies are actually naturally occurring hybrids of mountain poppy species. Sometimes Iceland poppies are referred to as *Papaver nudicaule*, but this plant is in reality an Asian species rare in cultivation. The Iceland poppies of gardens offer the tallest (to 24") and largest (3" to 6") flowers in the widest range of colors of the mountain poppy group — all but blue and purple — and are popular cut flowers in northern Europe. Many strains are available, including 'Garden Gnome' and 'Wonderland', two compact 10" to 12" selections, the latter available in single colors. 'Oregon Rainbows' offers the whole range of colors, as well as some bicolors and picotees; 'Champagne Bubbles' are more softly hued. Where summers are hot and winters mild, these plants make excellent winter and early spring flowers; in Texas they are often offered as tractable young transplants in the fall for just this purpose, lovely with wallflowers, hesperis and pansies before the heat sets in. Months later, the same glowing floral fireworks take place at much higher altitudes and more northerly latitudes: in regions where cool summers prevail, Iceland poppies provide a gay, breezy display from summer until early autumn.

Most poppies don't take up much room in the garden. This cannot be said for Oriental poppies, the striking 2' to 5' *Papaver orientale/P. bracteatum* selections and hybrids. While they have all the flashy looks of the poppy family and then some, their *modus operandi* is quite different. They have the dubious distinction of the shortest bloom time of any poppy, often but a week in late spring, yet the plants boast a longevity unmatched by most perennials. They draw more than their share of attention when in bloom, then demand a large area for their flaccid, bristly, basal foliage to elongate and finally go unceremoniously dormant in summer, leaving a botanical bomb crater in the garden. Yet that gargantuan 5" to 10" bowl of a flower hopelessly seduces the gardener. Replete with a fringe of dusky stamens, this fleeting floral flamenco dancer heralds the voluptuous bloom of late spring.

Oriental poppies are exceptionally winter-hardy, to USDA Zone 3, and actually require a cold winter to grow and bloom well. (For milder parts of California, the 'Minicap' series, a successful result of complex breeding, is best.) But they aren't fussy as far as soil is concerned, thriving even in heavy clay so long as it isn't waterlogged. The less rich the soil, the less likely the plant is to flop. By planting these robust, coarse poppies in the back of a border or deep within a planting, between equally bulky perennials, ornamental grasses and shrubs, the floppy stems have some support while weighted down by the huge blossoms, and later on the gaping hole left behind is less likely to be noticed. Choose the site with care; Oriental poppies can be moved, ideally in late summer, but the old site will not be truly vacated, for a new plant will undoubtedly sprout from even the tiniest bit of root left behind. In fact, 2" root cuttings are the most common means of propagation, sprouting vigorously in just four weeks.

Several times I have tried the recommended technique of pairing an Oriental poppy with a late-emerging perennial (baby's breath or *Aster ×frikartii*, for example) to disguise the summer gap, each time with less than satisfactory results. The poppy's vigorous spring growth always crowds the companion, weakening and disfiguring it. In climates where warm-season annuals grow quickly, such as the Middle Atlantic States and the Midwest, filling the early-summer gap with perilla, plectranthus, setcreasea and the like works much better.

Until the turn of the century, the only Oriental poppies available were orange red. That all changed when Amos Perry, a nurseryman near London, discovered salmon pink ('Mrs. Perry') and white ('Perry's White') forms. The choice today is great. Deep red cultivars include 'Beauty of Livermere', 'Warlord' and 'Goliath'. 'Harvest Moon' is a showy orange semidouble. For strong pink or rose, a popular selection is 'Raspberry Queen'. 'Princess Victoria Louise' is salmon; 'Betty Ann', 'Cedar Hill', and 'Queen Alexandra' offer softer pink tints. Fringed petals ('Türkenlouis' and 'Curlilocks') and several bicolors are to be had for exotic effects. Perhaps the most useful are the compact varieties, those that grow only 20" to 30" tall: pink 'Helen Elisabeth' and 'Juliane', red 'Allegro' and 'Rembrandt' and salmon 'Degas'. I had long been waiting for the enticing English cultivar 'Patty's Plum', purportedly discovered growing on the compost heap of the gardener after whom it was named, to come across the ocean into American trade. She finally arrived.

Tough Customers

Lastly, I want to advocate a neglected group of long-blooming, winter-hardy poppies — one biennial species and three perennials. All come embarrassingly easily from seed, transplant readily when small and have been among my top summer performers. They prefer a sunny, dry spot — a situation where most well-suited companions will have silver, sage-green, blue or gray foliage rather than the strong greens of a moister area. These soft

Papaver atlanticum

foliage colors work infinitely better with the poppies' orange, peach and apricot flowers. I think the pervasive dislike of orange in the garden is due to the strong, almost lurid, contrast between these colors and true green. But bring on the fuzzy chartreuse velvet of marrubiums, the powder blue of sheep's fescue, the silver and gray of artemisias, and suddenly orange looks sublime.

The biennial Armenian poppy (*Papaver triniifolium*) is worth growing for its foliage alone — a rosette of blue filigree that looks more like a doily than a cluster of leaves. In its second year, an 18" candelabrum of pale apricot flowers rises up, flowering for two months or more before setting a pound of viable seed and passing on.

Moroccan perennial *Papaver atlanticum* and its Spanish cousin *P. rupifragum* are almost identical, the latter having flowers more red than orange and foliage with less hair. Both have been perennial for six years or more in my garden, self-sowing here and there. They put forth dozens upon dozens of 15" to 20" stems with nodding buds that open into 2" flowers. The show continues from late spring into fall if the plants are periodically deadheaded. Semidouble forms of both species, called 'Flore Pleno', come true from seed. The delicate flowers are especially effective seen floating through a haze of June grass (*Koeleria micrantha*) or any other grass with flowers of similar height and texture.

The last and largest of the group is the elegant 2' *P. spicatum* (also listed as *P. heldreichii*), a long-lived Turkish perennial with the unusual habit of pressing its flowers closely along the stems. Hairy, sage-green foliage sets off 2" flowers in colors ranging from brick red through orange into exquisite icy peach, lovely with blue oat grass.

In the language of flowers, poppies signify forgetfulness. They don't seem to be heading toward oblivion anytime soon, however. While their self-sowing, casual ways may strike fear in the hearts of controlling gardeners, these gypsy girls of the garden will continue to enchant the rest of us with their complex beauty, at once familiar and exotic.

ORNAMENTAL RHUBARBS

with their bold foliage and plumy flowers, these unusual perennials can inspire a lifelong passion

by Daniel J. Hinkley

Rheum palmatum

Among those gardeners who have cultivated edible rhubarb (*Rheum ×hybridum*), there can be few who have not admired the plant's columns of white flowers as they unfurl in early summer. When I was young, I was often admonished never to let our old, hand-me-down clump of rhubarb blossom, for fear that it would be weakened if allowed to do so. Although I listened to this advice, fortunately, I didn't always heed it, for it was my youthful fondness for these curious, brawny, flowering stems that later led me to examine the magnificent genus *Rheum* in greater detail.

Certainly the best known of the ornamental rhubarbs is the Chinese species *R. palmatum*, most often encountered in its red-flowered form, *R. p.* 'Atrosanguineum'.

Rheum 'Ace of Hearts'

(All the rhubarbs discussed here are hardy to USDA Zone 5.) When the plant awakens in early spring, the young foliage is ruby red. As the jagged leaves enlarge, ultimately reaching nearly 3' across, the reddish tints of the upper leaf surfaces take on the patina of aged copper, while the undersides remain an intense, matte, rose red. This plant holds me spellbound in the early days of May, when its fresh leaves, backlit by the sun, display their arresting colors and textures. Then, in early June, a massive flowering stem heads skyward, carrying large, knobby buds sheathed in scarlet bracts. Once the stem has reached its maximum height (as much as 7'), the buds open into an airy spectacle of crimson flowers touched with cerise. If seed set is good, the plant provides yet another season of interest, with numerous glossy, red, triangular fruits dangling from the tree-like inflorescence. There are several named cultivars of this species, and though they are all exceptionally attractive, I have found that plants raised from seed can easily hold their own against them. Gardeners should bear in mind that the foliage of young plants is not as distinctively lobed or as colorful as that of mature specimens.

As fond as I am of using bold foliage as a contrast to more delicate leaves, mammoths such as *R. palmatum* can be difficult to incorporate into modest-size gardens. Fortunately, there are numerous smaller species and hybrids that still provide good foliar contrast. *Rheum australe*, for example, emerges in early spring with handsome, tawny pink leaves that expand ultimately to 1' or more while darkening to a rich green. From the tidy, low mound of foliage, a 4' flowering stem emerges bearing creamy white flowers. In my Seattle-area garden it grows next to *Hebe anomala*, which has needlelike, purplish, evergreen foliage — a good contrast to the rhubarb in both texture and color.

In the autumn of 1995, long after my fondness for this genus had ripened into infatuation, I found myself with four friends and 24 Sherpas on a high ridge in eastern Nepal called the Jajale Himal. Here, in the high Himalayas, we found two species of rhubarb. The first, *R. acuminatum*, is superbly worth cultivating both for its foliage and for its flowers. The 10", glistening green leaves are triangular in shape with a heavily veined texture, while the undersides of the leaves and the petioles are a bright cherry red.

In early summer, 3' flowering stems carry sprightly panicles of rose-red flowers, followed in most years by a crop of red fruits. Though this plant is native to alpine meadows at nearly 12,000 feet, it has settled down contentedly in my garden, growing in bright shade with asarums, hellebores, erythroniums and cyclamen.

The second species we encountered was the fabled Tibetan rhubarb, *R. nobile*, growing in large numbers by the side of a high-alpine lake at 15,000 feet. This almost surreal species produces rigid, pyramidal flowering stems that can reach 5', cloaked from top to bottom in 10", translucent, creamy pink and amber bracts, making the colony we saw look like a petrified army of strangely clad soldiers. Beneath the bracts (which protect the flowers from rain and frost), we found short panicles crowded with thousands of seeds — evidence of the plants' imminent demise, for *R. nobile* is monocarpic, storing up food reserves for several years and then flowering and setting seed only once before dying. Although the seed we collected germinated within weeks of returning home, I suspect this high-altitude species is best suited to extremely cool and moist climates, such as western Scotland or maritime Alaska.

Rheum alexandrae, a closely related species with similar protective bracts along the flowering stem, is much more amenable to cultivation, and has been blossoming in my garden since 1994. Native to the Tibetan plateau and the mountains of western China, it is soundly perennial, though I have found that it tends to flower only in alternate years. The distinctive, lance-shaped, 10", glossy green leaves form a low clump, from which the 2' flowering stems emerge in June. Each carries a series of translucent bracts, like creamy white hearts, along its entire length. As with *R. nobile*, the flowers of *R. alexandrae* are produced on short panicles hidden beneath the bracts. In the autumn of 1996, I found this species in the mountains of northwestern Yunnan Province growing in wet meadows and along the margins of lakes at elevations of 10,000 to 14,000 feet, its foliage turned to glossy clarets and oranges by the crisp October air. Interestingly, when I planted this species in perpetually moist spots in my own garden — conditions I thought would suit it perfectly — it invariably died. It wasn't until I tried it in full sun in a slightly raised bed that received supplemental irrigation during the summer that it began to thrive and blossom, although it hasn't exhibited the intense autumn foliage color that I observed in China.

Ideally suited to the rock garden or to the front of the border in full sun, *R. kialense* is among the smallest of the rhubarbs that I grow. This endearing plant forms spreading mounds of 4", triangu-

Rheum palmatum 'Atrosanguineum'

lar leaves with rose undersides. In early summer, small, red flowers appear in abundance on willowy, 8" stems. In my garden this species is paired with somewhat softer hues of *Veronica spicata* 'Rotfuchs'.

Rheum kialense is thought to be one of the parents of *R.* 'Ace of Hearts', a hybrid that is among the best foliage plants I have ever used in my perennial borders. It produces substantial mounds of heart-shaped leaves, whose burgundy-red undersides are in full view thanks to their stiffly upright posture. It has not flowered in my garden, nor have I heard of it flowering for others, but that is of no concern to me whatsoever. Paired with the rich lavender spikes of *Salvia pratensis* or flanking the golden foliage of *Philadelphus*

keeping your rhubarbs WELL-GROOMED

After their exuberant early-summer flowering, ornamental rhubarbs can look somewhat worse for the wear. Especially in parts of the country that experience late-spring hailstorms, that once-gorgeous foliage can beg for a makeover. This should be done at the end of June. Remove both the flowering stems and the foliage, and give each plant a handful of high-nitrogen fertilizer. Within days, the plants will respond with vigorous new foliage that will stay respectable until the first frosts.

coronarius 'Aureus', its foliage is unsurpassed, whether used as complement or contrast.

Another exceptional small species for a well-drained spot in full sun is *R. persicum*. Its 10", rounded, leathery, wrinkled leaves appear in early spring, forming a rather prostrate but still ornamental mound. From its center arises a 6"-high cluster of brick-red flowers that are attractive in a somewhat extraterrestrial way. In our garden it anchors a fairly dry bed that it shares with finely textured companions, including diascias, *Gaura lindheimeri* and the gray-leaved, powder-blue-flowered *Veronica turrilliana*.

Whether encountering rhubarbs in their native Asian haunts or simply viewing them in my own garden, my experience with these plants has been one of unalloyed pleasure. From an early curiosity, my relationship with the genus *Rheum* has deepened into a firm and abiding partnership. These splendid ornamentals are and will continue to be a cherished component of my garden.

propagating RHUBARB

Ornamental rhubarbs can be propagated by both division and seed. Division, however, can be daunting for beginners because the plants' root structures are quite woody. Before growth begins in early spring, look for dormant buds on the roots. Then, with a digging fork or sharp knife, remove a single bud along with a substantial piece of root. Replant it at the same depth at which it was growing. If you wish to propagate your plants by seed, harvest the seeds when they begin to fall from the flowering stem in midsummer. Sow the seed immediately; germination should be quick. The following spring, seedlings can be transplanted to containers or directly into the garden.

Rheum alexandrae

IMPROBABLE PEONIES

breeders have overcome genetic barriers to create these tough, gorgeous hybrids

by JAMES W. WADDICK

It seems that every group of plant hybridizers has its own impossible dream: for rosarians it's a blue rose; for bearded iris fanatics, a truly red iris.

For peony fanciers — at least for many decades — it was a deep yellow, large-flowered, easy-to-grow herbaceous peony. This seemingly unreachable goal, however, has been achieved; in fact, the earliest examples of these "improbable peonies" — which now come in a wide spectrum of sumptuous colors — are nearly 50 years old. Strangely, most gardeners are unaware of these desirable hybrids, even though they are available from specialty nurseries and are held in special esteem by devoted peony growers. Like all stories that involve beating the odds, theirs is a compelling one.

The Challenge

The first barrier to breeding a good yellow herbaceous peony was the dearth of genetic material among the possible candidates for parents. *Paeonia mlokosewitschii*, from the Caucasus Mountains of eastern Europe — the first yellow-flowered herbaceous species to be discovered — looked promising at first. Named in 1900, it was quickly brought into cultivation. Although fairly easy to grow and an attractive light yellow in its best forms, the flowers are single and short-lived. Furthermore, it proved disappointing as a parent, repeatedly failing to produce any good, bright yellow offspring.

Another candidate turned up during the Japanese occupation of northeastern China in the 1930s. Discovered blooming on the grounds of the last emperor's palace in Changchun, in the heart of Manchuria, it was a double-flowered yellow that went under the Chinese name 'Huang Jin Lun' (translated as "golden wheel"). It

was brought to Japan (where it became known as 'Yokihi') and introduced into cultivation. A series of circuitous and mysterious moves finally brought it to the United States in 1954, where it was registered as 'Oriental Gold'. For all the romance of its origin, it proved difficult to grow, harder to flower and expensive to boot. Moreover, its few hybrids were similarly disappointing.

An Elusive Goal

In contrast to the dearth of yellow herbaceous peonies, there were plenty of good yellows among tree peonies, thanks mainly to two species from western China: *Paeonia lutea*, discovered in 1884, and *P. delavayi*, discovered in 1921. Brought to Western Europe, these species grew well, bloomed, and created a sensation. Between the 1890s and 1930s the French hybridizer Victor Lemoine used *P. lutea* (along with *P. suffruticosa* and Japanese hybrids) to produce the first of the large, double-flowered "lutea hybrids," some of which, such as 'Alice Harding', 'Chromatella' and 'Souvenir de Maxime Cornu', are still in cultivation. These were probably the inspiration for a host of yellow-flowered tree peonies produced in the 1940s by the talented American hybridizer A. P. Saunders.

Now, if the superior floral qualities of the yellow-flowered tree peonies could be transferred to herbaceous peonies, the problem would be solved. But according to conventional wisdom, the genetic barriers between tree peonies and herbaceous peonies ruled out any attempts to cross the two groups. (See "The Different Kinds of Peonies," later in this chapter.) Conventional wisdom, however, turned out to be wrong.

1. 'Watermelon Wine' **2.** 'First Arrival' **3.** 'Unique' **4.** 'Scarlet Heaven'

5. 'Julia Rose' 6. A unnamed Roger Anderson hybrid 7. 'Pastel Splendor' 8. 'Cora Louise'

Success

In Japan, around 1948, an avid amateur gardener named Toichi Itoh applied the pollen of the yellow tree peony 'Alice Harding' to the Japanese herbaceous peony 'Kakoden' and obtained viable seeds. Most of the resulting seedlings looked like herbaceous peonies, but nine had foliage more typical of tree peonies. Eventually, all but six of these died. Sadly, Itoh himself also died in 1956, without ever seeing his "impossible" hybrids flower. Fortunately, Itoh's assistant kept the remaining six seedlings growing until they eventually flowered for the first time in 1963. All of them were short in stature, to about 20" and had large, deep-yellow, semidouble flowers; four of the best were registered in 1974 as 'Yellow Crown', 'Yellow Dream', 'Yellow Emperor', and 'Yellow Heaven'. (Some experts believe that these four have now become hopelessly mixed up in the trade.) The vigorous plants had the

attractive foliage of their tree peony parent while retaining the herbaceous nature and increased hardiness of their herbaceous parent. Their appearance set off a storm of further hybridizing attempts.

A minor furor arose over what to call the new peonies; on the one hand, there was a substantial body of opinion in favor of calling them "Itoh hybrids," in honor of their originator, but there were also many sensible arguments in support of the name "intersectional hybrids," because eventually a number of other species and hybrids unknown to Itoh were used in breeding these peonies. On balance, intersectional hybrids seems to be the most appropriate label.

Improving on Itoh

Repeating Itoh's success proved challenging. It was soon determined that not just any cross would work, and even then only a very few attempts resulted in fertile seeds. By the mid-1980s, however, several American breeders had managed to release new intersectionals. The first was nurseryman Don Hollingsworth, proprietor of Hollingsworth Peonies in Maryville, Missouri, whose hybrids 'Border Charm', 'Prairie Charm', and 'Garden Treasure' varied in the strength of their yellow coloration. 'Garden Treasure', however, a cross between the tree peony 'Alice Harding' and an unnamed herbaceous seedling, really threw down the gauntlet to other breeders. This plant was larger than the original Itohs, and had a better growth habit. The flowers can reach a full 8" in diameter, and are a bright, clear yellow with small red "flares" at the center. 'Garden Treasure' went on to receive the Gold Medal of the American Peony Society, and demand still far exceeds the supply.

The hybridizer Roger Anderson, owner of Callie's Beaux Jardins in Fort Atkinson, Wisconsin, then introduced more than 20 new intersectionals that have dramatically expanded the group's color range to include pink, white, lilac, orange, copper and bicolors. Outstanding among his yellows is 'Bartzella', an improvement in many ways on all other yellow-flowered peonies. It is an upright grower, reaching nearly 36" in height. The large (up to 8") flowers are a clean, bright yellow with small, central reddish flares, and practically cover the plant. 'Bartzella' is also fast growing and quickly reaches specimen size. Some fanciers consider it the world's most desirable peony.

pick of the best INTERSECTIONALS

NAME	BREEDER	DESCRIPTION
'Bartzella'	Anderson	semidouble, bright yellow, upright; a gem
'Cora Louise'	Anderson	semidouble white with a darker red center
'Garden Treasure'	Hollingsworth	semidouble yellow, spreading habit; award winner
'Julia Rose'	Anderson	single to semidouble flowers of red, orange, and yellow on one plant
'Morning Lilac'	Anderson	semidouble with bright lilac-pink flowers, darker in center
'Scarlet Heaven'	Anderson	single deep red flowers on a rounded bush
'Viking Full Moon'	Pehrson/Seidl	soft yellow rounded flowers on a 3' plant
'Yellow Crown'	Itoh	dwarf plant (to 20") with yellow flowers with red central flares
'Yellow Dream'	Itoh	see under 'Yellow Crown'
'Yellow Emperor'	Itoh	see under 'Yellow Crown'
'Yellow Heaven'	Itoh	see under 'Yellow Crown'

9. 'Bartzella', showing foliage and plant habit **10.** 'Bartzella'

patience. Seedlings take years to a decade to mature and produce their first bloom. Finally, propagating them is dauntingly slow. Intersectionals produce huge root systems, and their woody peony parentage means that they have tough stem bases and crowns; division, therefore, is laborious and produces relatively few new plants. (Tissue culture, unfortunately, doesn't work with peonies.)

Although achieving a good yellow was the original impetus behind the creation of the intersectionals, it is hard to resist some of Anderson's more novel colors. 'Kopper Kettle', for example, is a mix of red, yellow and orange, giving an overall orange/copper impression. 'Pastel Splendor' (introduced with W. Seidl) is mostly white but suffused with light pink and yellow, blending into a rich red center. 'Cora Louise' takes this a step further with near-white petals with contrasting lavender-purple central flares. 'First Arrival', the earliest of Anderson's intersectionals to bloom, is a full-flowered lavender pink on a perfectly formed bush. The unusual 'Julia Rose' opens cherry red, then fades to orange and near yellow. All three colors can be seen on one plant. Anderson's reds range from the pale 'Watermelon Wine' to the deep 'Scarlet Heaven' and the aptly named 'Unique', which inherited its finely cut foliage from the red-flowered woody species *P. delavayi*.

Although it's the flowers of Anderson's hybrids that grab your attention, he is justifiably proud of their attractive, long-lasting foliage, which looks almost as fresh in September as it does in May.

Beauty at a Price

Surely, you must be thinking, there's got to be a catch with these dazzling plants; otherwise they'd be flooding my local garden center. There is: they're expensive. 'Bartzella' sells for $250, while the award-winning 'Garden Treasure' is a relative bargain at $125. Most other intersectionals sell from $100 to $200 each. Why the astronomic prices? First of all, the crosses are difficult to make, demanding extreme

But once you've gotten over your sticker shock, you can't help but appreciate their sterling qualities. They are relatively trouble free, fast growing, and extremely hardy — to USDA Zone 3 or even 2. Most have an extended bloom season, and in mid-northern latitudes can last well into June. And any intersectional will be delightfully different from all the other peonies in your garden.

So what is in the future of these fantastic plants? It's likely that their color range will continue to expand, to pure white and exotic blends and bicolors. Also expect to see distinctive foliage, the possibility of repeat bloom in the fall, and fully fertile plants that will make breeding them less of a challenge. But more important, as they become better known and more intensively propagated, their price will surely fall, making these peonies of the future increasingly available to gardeners across the country.

the different kinds OF PEONIES

Peonies fall into three groups, or subgenera: the tree or woody peonies; the majority of herbaceous peonies; and the one or two American herbaceous peony species, which are of interest primarily to specialists. Tree peonies have been grown for centuries in Chinese and Japanese gardens. Although called "tree" peonies, none actually attain treelike proportions; woody peonies is a better term. Most cultivars stay under 6', but a few (such as 'Ludlowii') can grow to nearly double that size. All have woody stems that continue to grow over many years, and should be treated in the garden like other deciduous shrubs of similar size. Most are hardy to USDA Zone 4.

Herbaceous peonies have been grown in the West since ancient times both for medicinal and ornamental purposes. Hardier in general than woody peonies (to Zone 3), herbaceous peonies can grow to up to 4' or so in height, but die down in the fall to below ground level, where their dormant buds wait out winter's chill. They form the backbone of many gardens, ranking with other perennial favorites such as irises and daylilies. Yellow-flowered varieties are rare, and none are both a good yellow and easy to grow.

ANOTHER WORLD OF DAYLILIES

these plants, once treasured by gardeners for their elegance of form, are mostly unknown today

by BETTY GATEWOOD

Most gardeners who think they know daylilies know (and grow) modern hybrids, the plants that specialist breeders have produced by the thousands.

'Neyron Rose' (left) and 'Evelyn Claar' (right; both 1950)

'Ophir' (1924)   'Canari' (1940)   'Swansdown' (1951)

Prized by collectors for their ever-larger flowers, their splashy color combinations, their ruffles, watermarks, halos, picotee edges and other elaborations, these are the daylilies most sought after today.

But there is another world of daylilies — that of species and early hybrids. These plants, once treasured by gardeners for their elegance of form, are mostly unknown today, even among specialists. Species and early hybrids come in a simple range of colors — think of oranges and lemons, yellow pencils, school buses and the Kodak box — and they have few of the striking features that today's collectors crave. But they are distinguished by one great quality: They retain the classic lily shape that has largely been bred out of modern daylilies. They are supremely beautiful. For this alone they are worth seeking out.

I was introduced to old daylilies in 1986 by an encounter with a book called *Daylilies* (originally published in 1934) by the botanist Arlow Burdette Stout. At the time, I thought I didn't much like daylilies. Except for a clump of 'Hyperion', a classic yellow from 1925 that is still available today, most of the daylilies I had grown didn't fit in with the rest of my garden. They were too big and too showy, out of scale with my assortment of campanulas, cranesbills, irises, alliums, salvias, and other lacy, billowy, cottage-garden perennials. And often when I planted one, its color — especially if pink or red — fought with the flowers that surrounded it. I ended up giving many daylilies away. But when I saw the fuzzy gray photos of Dr. Stout's book, I was captivated. His daylilies looked like lilies, and they were smaller and shapelier than most daylilies I knew. Although the photos were black and white, Stout's descriptions of strong, clear colors — lemon yellow and rich golden orange — were beguiling.

After some searching through mail-order catalogs (this was be-fore the days of the Internet) I ordered three of these daylilies: *Hemerocallis flava*, a species now known as *H. lilioasphodelus*, and the hybrids 'Gold Dust' and 'Orangeman', which date from before 1906 (exactly when is unknown). All three bloomed the following May (yes, May) and immediately made me a collector of old daylilies.

Daylily Species

All daylilies are natives of Asia — primarily of China, Japan, and Korea — where they have long been used for medicine and food. We know from botanical illustrations that plants had been brought to Europe by the 16th century. Linnaeus identified two species: *H. fulva* (tawny orange, the familiar roadside specimen) and *H. flava* (yellow). Most other species recognized today were identified in the 18th and 19th centuries as explorers and plant hunters brought them back from their expeditions to Asia, primarily China. By 1900, more than a dozen species were recognized, but confusion reigned, as nomenclature was inconsistent and many species had variant forms.

Enter Dr. Stout, who arrived at the New York Botanical Garden in 1911. He worked diligently to identify and classify the species, but his 1934 book bears ample witness to his difficulty: "The species of daylilies are variable and . . . there are several different plants in culture under each of the names." This confusion persists today, but botanists now recognize around 20 species (exactly how many depends on which botanist you ask), and new species (and variants) are still being discovered.

All daylily species bear yellow, gold, or orange flowers. The reds, pinks and purples seen in modern daylilies are the result of hybridizing from one variant, pink-tinged form of the tawny daylily, *H. fulva*, brought back from China in the 1920s. Species flowers

Large vase (left to right): 'Golden Chalice' (1943), 'Green Gold' (1951), and 'Sceptre' (1946). Small vase (left to right): 'Corky' (1959) and 'Golden Chimes' (1954).

Every gardener who has an interest in heirloom plants must learn to live with mystery. Accumulating a foundling patch — a collection of the nameless — is inevitable. I have chosen daylilies from nurseries where labels were missing or growers couldn't identify their stock. I have bought unregistered (and thus nameless) seedlings. I have been sent plants in the mail that have proved to be not what I ordered. I've begged plants from friends who could only tell me, "it was here when we bought the house."

Gardeners who want to identify old daylilies can find help from the Hemerocallis Check List 1893–1957, published by the American Hemerocallis Society. For more information, visit www.daylilies.org.

Unknown hybrid, possibly 'Dr. Slaughter'   Unknown hybrid

have narrow petals and are distinctly lily- or trumpet-shaped. Species plants, however, vary greatly in size (from less than 6" to more than 6') and period of bloom (from early May to late September). Some flower at night, and some hold their flowers open for more than a day, a phenomenon known as extended blooming. Hybrids from the species often carry their parents' characteristics.

I grow several species in my garden, among them *H. citrina, H. dumortieri, H. hakunensis, H. lilioasphodelus, H. middendorffii, H. multiflora,* and *H. yezoensis* — or at least I think I do. Plants offered for sale as species may not be, and it is difficult to be sure without consulting a botanist, or several. Gardeners who choose to grow them must be able to tolerate some uncertainty and to enjoy them for what they are — beautiful plants. Those for whom a plant's identity is important might prefer to grow early named hybrids, which have all the qualities of the species and (sometimes) a clearer pedigree.

Early Hybrids

Although Dr. Stout's name is preeminent among early hybridizers, the first recognized hybrid, 'Apricot' (1893), was the creation of George Yeld (1845–1953), a British schoolmaster who grew daylilies as a hobby. Yeld also bred or recorded the existence in the trade of 'Sovereign', 'Gold Dust', 'Estmere', and 'Orangeman', all of which date from around

1906. These daylilies are very early, blooming the second or third week of May in my garden, and all are fragrant. Except for 'Sovereign', which is yellow, all are gold and fairly short (around 30" or less).

By the time of Dr. Stout's book (1934), a few hundred hybrids had been produced, and many of these had become commercially available. Unfortunately, many have been lost over the years, and others probably still circulate with inaccurate names or no names at all. I have located and grown about 30 of the more than 150 cultivars described in the book and chosen to keep about 20 for my own garden. Of these, the only well-known cultivar is 'Hyperion' (1925), a pale yellow, slightly fragrant July bloomer that is still widely available. Unfortunately, many other yellow daylilies travel under the name of 'Hyperion'; the problem of misnamed plants is still very much with us.

Daylily fanciers today usually dismiss varieties such as 'Hyperion' as historical curiosities of limited interest. The oldies, they believe, have been superseded by varieties with larger, showier flowers, sturdier stems, longer blooming periods or other perceived advantages. Since my criterion is a simple one — beauty of form — I consider none of these qualities an advantage. A daylily like 'Ophir' (1924), for example, has large trumpet-shaped flowers (rather like a golden orange Easter lily) of unmatchable shape. It is also a robust grower, tall (about 4'), slightly fragrant and very

'Orangeman' (EE)

H. middendorffii (EE)

'Autumn Minaret' (MLa)

H. multiflora (VLa)

'Autumn Prince' (MLa)

'Aureole' (EM)

H. dumortieri (EE)

EE: Extra Early

EM: Early Midseason

MLa: Late Midseason

VLa: Very Late

H. yezoensis (left) and H. hakunensis (right)

'Linda' (left; 1937) and 'Poinsettia' (right; 1953)

floriferous. Blooming around the third week of June and continuing for almost a month, it is far too fine a plant to be forgotten — fully the equal of the better-known 'Hyperion'.

Near contemporaries of 'Ophir', such as the delicate yellow 'Gracilis' (1933) — little more than 1' tall, with thin, grassy foliage — are also worth growing. 'Flava Major' (pre-1925) is also yellow, much larger in every dimension, and strongly fragrant. 'Aureole' (1918), golden orange and floriferous, is another early-flowering standout. Most of these very old hybrids are the offspring of species such as *H. lilioasphodelus* and *H. dumortieri* that bloom in late spring. In my garden, their peak bloom comes around May 20, and their clear, bright yellows and golds combine well with the mostly cool colors that prevail then — from lavender bearded iris, blue and white Siberian iris, many geraniums (*G. pratense*, *G. sylvaticum*, *G. ×magnificum*, *G. macrorrhizum* and others), columbines, white dame's rocket, *Anchusa azurea* and various amsonias. The background of intense green from the foliage of many later-blooming perennials makes all these colors compatible. Visitors to my garden in late May invariably ask, "Are those daylilies?" The amount of bloom, and its exuberant marigold palette so early in the year are a shock to those who expect daylilies only in July.

Developments in Hybridization

Beginning in the 1920s, new *Hemerocallis* species arrived at the New York Botanical Garden, and Dr. Stout sought not only to classify them botanically but to use their characteristics in his hybridization program. From *H. fulva* var. *rosea*, he took pinkish pigment that eventu-

ally allowed him to produce the first pink and red daylilies in 1934. From *H. multiflora*, a species from China, he took branching stature and late-blooming habit, and from *H. altissima* he took enormous height — 6' or more.

Today, a number of Dr. Stout's creations can still be found in the trade. Although they are admirable, I find them difficult to place in my own garden because so many are red, hot orange or tawny, but I do like the shocking 'Buckeye' (1941), an early gold with a maroon eye, 'Poinsettia' (1953), a midseason red with perfect form and delicate markings, and its companions 'Linda' (1937), a cream and light orange bitone, and 'Serenade' (1937), a spidery orange with a pale stripe. Best of all, however, are the late-season *H. altissima* hybrids, in particular the lemon yellow 'Autumn King' (1950) and the shorter but similar 'Autumn Prince' (1941). I wait all summer for the first buds to open on these very tall plants ('Prince' reaches nearly 4', 'King' close to 6') at the turn of August. They are ideal companions for bronze fennel and for late white flowers — phlox, *Euphorbia corollata* and *Veronicastrum virginicum*, all of which also offer contrasting foliage. They continue to bloom until nearly the end of September, and are faintly fragrant.

By the 1940s and 1950s, a number of hybridizers were producing wonderful daylilies, but today most of their names are familiar only to daylily fanciers. One such hybridizer was Elizabeth Nesmith of Massachusetts, a contemporary of Dr. Stout. I grow only one of her creations, 'Canari' (1940), but it is such a beautiful thing that I will be grateful to her for as long as I garden. A creamy pale yellow with a spidery shape, it grows to about 3' and flowers in mid-July.

Another great creation is David Hall's 'Swansdown' (1951), which strongly resembles 'Hyperion' but is a much paler yellow. In this era breeders produced hundreds, perhaps thousands, of such cultivars that have been all but forgotten today. Other favorites in my midseason collection are 'Golden Chalice' (1943), a forthright gold and a powerful grower; 'Sceptre' (1946), another gold of classic form; 'Libby Finch' (1949), a starry red with a cream stripe; and 'Green Gold' (1951), a bright yellow with a greenish cast. Two small-flowered varieties, 'Golden Chimes' (1954) and 'Corky' (1959), provide an interesting contrast to the larger midseason crowd. With a few exceptions, my choices are yellow and gold, with a few reds, because these blend in best with the rest of my garden. Most older pink daylilies have a distinct tawny undertone that makes them impossible to combine with clear or bluish pinks. I do keep two old pinks of good form, 'Neyron Rose' and 'Evelyn Claar' (both 1950) in a corner of their own, surrounded by greenery.

Why Grow Them?

Given the thousands of daylilies on the market, why grow these antiques? Modern daylilies are everywhere; by contrast, species and old hybrids can be hard to find. Besides their beauty, old daylilies have other fine qualities. Many are fragrant. Their thinner, smaller flowers mean that deadheads are not very noticeable — in contrast to modern daylilies, which are disfigured by heavy, ugly spent blooms. (Since flowers open only for a day, this is not a trivial consideration: Modern daylilies must be deadheaded daily or they look slovenly.) The old varieties range widely in size and in bloom time — daylilies flower in my garden from mid-May until the end of September, sometimes longer. Their colors are clear and stable; they combine well and most suffer little weather damage. They are vigorous and naturalize well in areas where deer are not a problem. And they are inexpensive, often as little as a few dollars per plant. (My superb 'Canari' cost $3 in 1994.)

And their disadvantages? Their flowers are mostly smaller, and their color range is limited — if you abhor yellow and gold flowers, look elsewhere. Certainly, most are not as showy or as elaborate as modern hybrids, and they lack the unusual color combinations and baroque forms breeders seek today. Some can lean or flop; their stems are not as thick (I would say coarse) as those of modern varieties, especially tetraploids. Some, like my favorite 'Swansdown,' have imperfect foliage, undistinguished and limp (my love for that ethereal flower makes me tolerate the leaves). And some modern varieties bloom longer — but I would rather have three weeks of a flower I love than months of one that is commonplace.

Although I've been exploring old daylilies now for more than 15 years, I am always on the lookout for new varieties to collect, wishing only that more gardeners might join me in admiring plants that should not disappear.

for further **READING**

Daylilies, by A.B. Stout (Macmillan, 1934; reprinted with an introduction and updating by Darrel Apps, Sagapress, 1986)
Hemerocallis, by Walter Erhardt (Kangaroo Press, 1992)
A Passion for Daylilies, by Sydney Eddison (HarperCollins, 1992)
The Gardener's Guide to Growing Daylilies, by Diana Grenfell (Timber Press, 1998)
Hemerocallis Check List 1893–1957 (American Hemerocallis Society)

FROM UMBEL ROOTS

the carrot family offers an extraordinary array of attractive flowers

by DANIEL J. HINKLEY

Astrantia major 'Sunningdale Variegated'

Eryngium planum

Hacquetia epipactis

As plant families go, there are few whose members are as superficially similar as the *Umbelliferae*, commonly known as the carrot family (now known to botanists as the *Apiaceae*).

In fact, the familial relationship between this congregation of herbs and shrubs was recognized by the early Greeks long before the advent of modern plant taxonomy, making it the first acknowledged plant family. The words "umbellifer" and "umbrella" both derive from the same Latin root, which makes sense when one considers that the flowers of all members of the family are arranged in bumbershoot fashion, with the pedicels radiating outward from a common point of attachment to form a flat-topped inflorescence that is ideally suited as a landing platform for pollinating insects. From the ranks of this family come numerous species that are well known by gardeners and nongardeners alike. Carrots, caraway, parsley and parsnips are all part of the gang, yet there are many others possessing an ornamental flair that goes well beyond culinary use. With 4,000-odd species to choose from, it is easy to nominate a few that deserve more recognition as top-notch, durable and beguiling additions to our perennial borders. (All the plants discussed here are hardy to USDA Zone 5.)

Well over a decade ago, I was given a small plant of *Chaerophyllum hirsutum* 'Roseum' by a keen gardening friend in Seattle. Over time, my nursery staff and I have divided it so frequently that I am convinced that every gardener in North America must own it by now. Yet every spring as it comes into flower, visitors inquire as to the identity of this "rarity" and, more often than not, go home with a pot for their own gardens. After the emergence of the low, spreading mounds of handsome, deeply dissected foliage, the flattened, lacy heads of rose-colored flowers appear for weeks atop 15" stems. Consorting well with early tulips, it is one of the earliest performers in our spring borders, and I find it an endearing, tough, much-too-little-known perennial for full sun and a well-drained site.

Superficially, *Pimpinella major* 'Rosea', is very similar to *Chaerophyllum hirsutum*, though it comes into flower much later in the year (July to August) and grows substantially taller. Atop sturdy stems to 3' are produced lovely discs of light pink that are as good for cutting as they are simply left nestled mid-border in full sun. Because we cut this back hard directly after flowering, it pairs well with asters, which fill the void left behind.

Pimpinella major 'Rosea'

Astrantia major 'Hadspen Blood'

Certainly not all umbellifers require full sun; in fact, a large contingent need the cool, moist soils of woodland conditions. In our own garden, beneath a high overstory of Douglas firs, we grow many members of this vast family for both a dash of highly textural foliage as well as a lengthy and heady display of flowers that brighten what would be an otherwise dreary spot.

The genus *Astrantia*, whose members are commonly known as masterworts, is a supremely important ingredient of our shaded garden for its enormously long blooming season. Interestingly, the flowers of this genus do not outwardly resemble most other members of the Apiaceae. The tight clusters of blossoms are surrounded by persistent, papery, jagged-edged bracts that can easily be mistaken for petals. Because these bracts do not drop after flowering, their effect in the garden is long-lasting. For months on end, the flowers of *A. major* subsp. *involucrata* 'Shaggy', surrounded by these 2", white, green-tipped appendages, are presented on 15" stems above clumps of handsome, deeply lobed leaves. There are also several other infinitely gardenworthy selections of *Astrantia* that repay any effort to find them. *Astrantia major* 'Hadspen Blood' and *A. m.* 'Ruby Wedding' are English cultivars selected for their deep claret-colored bracts and flowers. 'Sunningdale Variegated' possesses white flowers held above foliage jauntily streaked with creamy white. Though the masterworts are adaptable to full sun in moist, well-drained positions, we find the floral effects last longer in somewhat shaded, cooler sites.

Somewhat similar in appearance is another European plant, *Hacquetia epipactis*, which makes a brilliant addition to our lightly shaded borders in late winter and early spring. Small, green, buttonlike clusters of flowers surrounded by shocking green bracts emerge in tight clusters that arise directly from ground level before the foliage appears. Eventually, the flowering stems lengthen to 6", while a lusty mound of lobed leaves gradually envelops the now-fading floral display. There is a dazzling variegated form of this plant known as 'Thor', though unfortunately it is seldom found in commerce.

The sea hollies, members of the genus *Eryngium*, are yet another branch of the family whose ornamental qualities are furnished by the bracts that surround the minute flowers. A biennial species, *E. giganteum*, is a startling, self-sowing stalwart with glossy, somewhat thistlelike foliage that rises to nearly 2' during its second year, offering as a swan song large, conical, greenish white flowers surrounded by prominent, ghostly white, sharply spined, leaflike structures. *Eryngium alpinum* is a dependable perennial species and a favorite of mine. The finely filigreed bracts emerge in shades of lime green, eventually changing to an intense midnight blue, and later still ripening to tawny brown. Unlike most other *Eryngium* species, however, the bracts only appear sharp; in reality they are quite feathery to the touch. Another perennial species, *E. planum*, is best known through numerous selections that have been made by the European cut-flower industry, one of which is the indispensable *E. lanum* 'Fluela'. Long-lasting, rickly textured, dazzling blue heads are held atop tall, sturdy stems that take on a similar hue as the flowers open.

Chaerophyllum hirsutum 'Roseum'

In a moist, bright bed in our woodland we grow two umbellifers side by side — one New World, one Old — whose effects could not possibly be more different. Our plants of *Selinum tenuifolium* came from seed that I collected at 14,000 feet in eastern Nepal in 1995. The frilly, dramatically dissected, fernlike foliage is carried on burgundy-colored stems rising to 4' that are capped in late summer by elegant, lacy heads of white flowers. I remain as captivated by this species now as I was on that crisp, late-autumn day in the Himalayas when I first observed it in its native haunts.

Its New World garden comrade is miles apart in appearance, and certainly among the most exciting new perennials currently under evaluation in our garden — for hardiness as well as invasive potential. *Mathiasella bupleuroides* was collected in the mountains of northeastern Mexico by the keen plantsmen of Yucca Do Nursery in Waller, Texas, and shared with us by Roger Raiche, a superb California plantsman, who grew it to perfection in his former garden in the hills of Berkeley, California. This species does not possess the foliar texture of *Selinum tenuifolium*, brandishing instead compound leaves to 2.5' composed of large, glossy leaflets. In flower, however, the effect is one of pure wonder: reminiscent of the flowers of the stinking hellebore, *Helleborus foetidus*, the nodding, compound umbels are subtended by jade-green bracts on stems rising to 6'. Perennial thus far in our Zone 8 climate, this might be better suited to pot culture in less accommodating parts of the country.

Unfortunately, numerous species within the *Apiaceae* possess characteristics that, while tempting to the gardener, are potentially perilous. For example, the giant hogweed, *Heracleum mantegazzianum*, is indeed impressive in flower, with table-size, creamy white umbels produced atop an almost treelike framework. But this species has proven to be extremely invasive in many parts of the country; moreover, photoreactive irritants found in its sap can cause serious physical harm to those trying to eradicate it (or simply cultivate around it). Another culprit is a seductively beautiful form of *Anthriscus sylvestris* with chocolate-colored foliage known as 'Ravenswing'; the species, however, has been placed on the Federal Noxious Weed List. With so many wanting to try this astounding plant, the potential for a "superinfection" of the species across the country is quite high. Though bishop's weed, *Aegopodium podagraria*, may not pose a threat to natural landscapes, anyone who has made the mistake of including this in their garden knows how virtually impossible it is to eradicate once established. As exciting as it is to trial new plants in our gardens, we must be alert to the danger that our passions may have an adverse effect on our continent's natural landscapes.

Fortunately, the list of potentially invasive plants among the *Apiaceae* is relatively small. The umbellifers present us with a throng of vastly underknown and sensational species that, in both foliage and flower, can bring months of pleasure to our gardens.

Eryngium giganteum

Astrantia major subsp. *involucrata* 'Shaggy'

chapter two
PERENNIALS FOR
special conditions

DRESSING UP FOR WINTER

the right plants can brighten the darkest season

by ANN LOVEJOY

Bronzed and brown, slumping in graceful fatigue, our plants are drifting off to their gentle winter sleep.

This twilight of the garden has a magic of its own, touched both by melancholy and the promise of renewal. By early winter the garden's bones are stripped bare and strengths of design or lapses of balance are revealed.

No matter where we garden, it is possible to create islands of continued interest within those slumbering beds by using off-season performers. Where winter is short and mild, as in USDA Zones 8 and 9, such winter vignettes are easy to orchestrate. A host of hardy, broad-leaved evergreens can form the basis for the island clusters, aided by one of the many winter-blooming perennials and bulbs. One of my favorite winter vignettes centers on large clumps of red-twigged dogwood, *Cornus alba* 'Sibirica' (USDA Zone 2; to 10'), whose rosy stems glow in soft winter light. Since young stems produce the best color, mature plants can be selectively thinned by a third each year and cut hard in spring to encourage strong new growth for next winter. Behind the dogwood glimmer arching wands of a thicketing whitewashed bramble, *Rubus cockburnianus* (Zone 6; to 10'). This long-stemmed Chinese beauty gleams against dim backdrops, and its icy white stems hold their own against the glitter of snow. Rose red and snow white mingle in delightful tangles, underplanted by curvaceous tussocks of coppery *Carex comans* 'Bronze Form' (Zone 7; to 16") in one setting and yellow-and-cream-striped *Carex morrowii* 'Variegata' (Zone 6; to 15") in another.

In a sheltered corner of my Zone 8 garden, a lusher, more flowery winter composition snuggles beneath *Rhododendron* 'Sir Charles Lemon' (Zone 7; slowly to 50'). This arboreal evergreen boasts long, leathery leaves with copper-felted undersides that luminesce warmly in gray winter twilight. At its feet, *Helleborus orientalis* subsp. *abchasicus* Early Purple Group (Zone 5; to 14") opens its nodding burgundy bells between November and March. Above them dangle the heavily tasseled fronds of a regal crested wood fern, *Dryopteris cristata* 'The King' (Zone 4; to 3'). Planted behind the rhododendron and threading through its lower limbs, the rather scraggly winter honeysuckle *Lonicera fragrantissima* (Zone 5; to 8') blooms from January through March, the fruity scent of its small, creamy flowers blending deliciously with the vanilla-and-honey fragrance of sweet box, *Sarcococca hookeriana* var. *humilis* (Zone 6; to 20"). This dapper little evergreen is encircled with snow crocuses (*C. chrysanthus*) that open in watercolor shades of blue from January into April.

Even with a less exotic plant palette, it is still quite possible to make pockets of visual pleasure where winter blows harsh and lingers long. In such climes, most winter vignettes quite rightly center on berry, bark and naked silhouettes. Though rarely considered winter-garden candidates, certain plants contribute surprisingly well simply through their shape. Unpruned hydrangeas, for instance, are enchanting under snow, their battered elegance restored to freshness by each fall of flakes. Spiky whorls of Adam's needle, *Yucca filamentosa* (Zone 4; to 3'), contrast powerfully with the stonelike shapes of

Euonymus europaeus 'Red Cascade'

Yucca filamentosa 'Bright Edge'

Pieris japonica 'Variegata'

anonymous, mounded shrubs. Dozens of grasses maintain a potent presence in winter, their tattered leaves rustling musically in the wind. Left unclipped, a wide range of border plants, from tall sedums to candytuft, look intriguing beneath their wintry white blanket.

In many places, however, snow is a sometime thing. When the garden is a frozen waste for endless bleak months, winter interest seems a poor joke. Where desiccating winds make even the toughest broad-leaved evergreens look ratty, the most reliable winter effects will come from conifers. Needled evergreens look dapper and lustrous in winter, when their sleek, fluffy coats seem thicker and glossier than ever. Cedars, firs, hemlocks, junipers, pines and yews can all be had in an enormous variety of sizes and shapes, introducing a vocabulary of form with which to furnish the coldest gardens.

Where the winter palette is narrow, it is helpful to take our lead from nature. Throughout the northernmost states, native plantings are quietly lovely in winter. The bare bones of trees rise like living pillars, their naked arms making lacework against leaden skies. Woodland floors are decorated with a spare elegance reminiscent of Asiatic gardens, where stones, ferns and mosses combine in understated arrangements of subtle beauty. Strong, simple designs based on repeated shapes and contrasts between massed plants and architecturally bold ones will carry best where winters are bitter.

In the middle states, where most gardens are in Zones 5, 6 or 7, rather more may be attempted. The place to begin building winter interest is wherever the sun lingers longest. Here, the first snowdrops and snow crocuses will appear long before those in the proper beds. If the palette of broad-leaved evergreens is modest, it is extended by a handful of hardy perennials and bulbs with which to weave more complex winter tapestries. In the cold Massachusetts garden of my youth, I loved to sip hot cocoa in the snow, perched in the sheltering lower branches of an enormous *Rhododendron catawbiense* (Zone 4; slowly to 18'). This flowered party-dress pink in June, but in winter its broad green leaves were smothered under snow blossoms.

Beneath its wide skirts, a scattering of evergreen Christmas ferns (*Polystichum acrostichoides*; Zone 3; to 3') punctuated a low ruffle of wintergreen or checkerberry, *Gaultheria procumbens* (Zone 3; to 5"). This mat of tangled greenery was studded with red berries that tasted sweet and faintly minty. Beloved of mice, plants in the woods were stripped by late fall, but here I could always find a berry or two in December. In smaller gardens, any of the hundreds of hardy, compact hybrid rhododendrons would happily fill a winter corner, similarly sheltering a sweep of white-flowered *Helleborus niger* (Zone 3; to 18") and long-flowering rose or garland daphne, *Daphne cneorum* (Zone 4; to 8"), interplanted with snowdrops and early scillas.

Beside my childhood rhododendron grotto, a European spindle tree (*Euonymus europaeus*; Zone 3; to 20') was always spangled with persistent hot pink and orange fruits in winter. This pleasant small tree has numerous attractive forms with similar wintry virtues, as do several of its relatives. Dainty Chinese winterberry, *E. bungeanus* (Zone 4; to 18'), is an open, airily constructed little tree whose delicate arms are decked in winter

Cyclamen coum

with copious quantities of bright red seeds spilling from tawny or rosy pods. Their cheerful glow is echoed by ruddy-stemmed dogwoods, such as coral-barked *Cornus alba* 'Westonbirt' (Zone 3; to 10') and the rich, reddish tatters of paperbark maple, *Acer griseum* (Zone 5; to 30').

An evergreen spindle relative, wintercreeper (*Euonymus fortunei*; Zone 5; vine or subshrub to 3') comes in a bewildering abundance of forms, plain and variegated, large of leaf or finely textured, climbing, scrambling or shrubby. Given decent garden soil, light shade and adequate summer moisture, the wintercreepers are handsome and adaptable plants with beauties in every season. In winter, the shrubby sorts like silver-edged 'Emerald Gaiety' and multicolored 'Emerald 'n' Gold' glow brilliantly in thin sunshine. Partnered with compact rhododendrons and dwarf kalmias, they will solidly anchor clusters of hardy ferns and hellebores.

Evergreen kalmias are invaluable in colder gardens, where their small, matte leaves and upright habit contrast pleasingly with the form and texture of conifers. Mountain laurel, *Kalmia latifolia* (Zone 4; 12'–30'), is a slow grower outside its native range and everywhere insists upon acid soil, but blooms young and remains neat and shapely from youth to maturity. Recent hybrids have broadened the range of flower color and form, so that gardeners who don't care for the washy pink of the species can select white or rose or red or even dull purple blossoms instead. A compact cousin,

sheep laurel (*K. angustifolia*; Zone 2; to 5'), thrives almost anywhere, but looks most at home in naturalistic gardens. In my Massachusetts garden, it was underplanted with Job's tears, *Coix lacryma-jobi*, a reseeding annual grass whose plump little seed heads resemble tiny cowrie shells glazed in gray lacquer. In winter, the wispy grass bent low under its burden of glossy beads.

The andromedas are equally desirable in winter vignettes, where their tidy good looks support less structural companions. Mountain andromeda, *Pieris floribunda* (Zone 4; 6'–8'), and Japanese andromeda, *P. japonica* (Zone 5; 8'–10'), are both mannerly, fairly slow growers that look their best when given protection from biting winter winds and baking summer sun. Dappled summer shade suits them best, and a great number of woodland plants will happily share their ground space. Hardy *Cyclamen coum* (Zone 6; to 4") seem to enjoy a rather rooty position at the feet of shrubs and trees. Often summer dormant, their fat corms produce their marbled or spotted new foliage in fall, followed in winter and spring by flocks of fluttering flowers in shades of rose, pink, cream and white. Striped and spotted lungworts, such as white-edged *Pulmonaria angustifolia* 'Variegata' (Zone 3; to 10"), silver-splashed *P.* 'Margery Fish' (Zone 3; to 1') or frosted *P.* 'Highdown' make pretty patterns even in the dead of winter, for though the old leaves look ragged and worn, the tight crowns begin to produce new foliage with the New Year.

This season of change is a good one in which to begin exploring the ways our winter gardens might be enriched. Though the year may be coming to an end, the garden need not die with it. Indeed, it never really does, for slow, minute changes are occurring every day, from the winter solstice on into spring. If we remain alive to the garden's subtle changes during the darkest days, we are ourselves renewed in its renewal.

Rubus cockburnianus

COPING WITH DRY SHADE

the right plants can green up even the most inhospitable corner

by Ann Lovejoy

Creating a green haven in dry shade ranks among garden-making's greatest challenges. While shade itself is far from a liability, the combination of deep shade and dry, often rooty soil presents even the most skilled gardener with significant difficulties.

Altering the environment may be our initial response, and indeed, simple changes can dramatically improve growing conditions. A program of soil improvement is essential for providing nourishment for roots in a competitive environment. Judicious thinning of tree branches brings more light to persistently dark places. (When the darkness comes from walls, light-reflective white paint and mirrors will maximize the available light.) It is equally important, of course, to select plants that have proven adaptable to such tough conditions. By altering the growing environment and choosing appropriate plants, the resourceful gardener can achieve exciting results.

To discover what will succeed in your dry, shady garden, look at what grows happily in your local woods. Towering firs, cedars, and madronas intermingled with alders and maples surround my northwestern garden. In the dry shade at the trees' feet grow glossy, evergreen mahonias and leathery salal, evergreen and deciduous huckleberries, rosy currant and bird-sown hollies. Beneath the shrubs' branches runs a host of perennials, from robust coltsfoot, false Solomon's seal, and sword ferns to dainty trilliums and tiny orchids. In New England woods I would find elderberry, witch hazel and dogwoods, dolls' eyes and fox grape, mayapples and wake robins, while the Deep South offers mountain laurel and azaleas, bowman's root and wild ginger. We can look farther afield as well, choosing woodland plants from all over the temperate world. The English woods provide additional inspiration with their famous bluebells, as do the magnificent mountain woods of eastern Europe and Asia, including the Himalayas.

Whatever their provenance, woodland plants have similar needs. All tolerate or even require shade and compete well for nutrients in crowded settings. Most have low or seasonal water requirements, generally preferring to be wet in winter and spring and dry in summer. Many bloom early or late in the year, when the leaf canopy is thin or nonexistent, and experience most of their active growth in fall, winter (when roots flourish), and early spring, going dormant as summer heats up. Shade gardeners soon discover that, because most woodland wildflowers are early bloomers, it takes some effort to develop an extended flowering season. The solution

Milium effusum 'Aureum'

Ajuga reptans 'Catlin's Giant'

Epimedium ×versicolor 'Sulphureum'

Dicentra 'Luxuriant'

is to expand the palette of plants to include a variety of evergreen or semievergreen shrubs and perennials that will help plantings look furnished at all times.

Shrubs

Small or large evergreen shrubs provide a sturdy backbone for any planting, and many of them tolerate dry shade with aplomb. The false cypress clan (*Chamaecyparis* spp.) offers numerous fine forms, notably selections of western Lawson cypress (*C. lawsoniana*; USDA Zone 5). These come in a great range of sizes (from 6' to 60') and colors, shading from rich greens through icy blues and grays to clear yellow and old gold. They will not tolerate deep and lasting drought, but given decent soil, summer irrigation and light or partial shade, many forms of this western native make fast-growing, handsome trees or shrubs.

Creeping Siberian false cypress (*Microbiota decussata*; Zone 2; 18" high by 6' wide) is a slow-growing conifer that broadens decorously in shade, where its toasty winter color looks warm and choco-

laty beside greener companions. This shaggy sprawler appreciates well-drained soils and grows happily in sun or quite deep shade.

Both butcher's broom (*Ruscus aculeatus*; Zone 7; to 4 ft.) and the similar-looking Alexandrian laurel (*Danae racemosa*; Zone 8; to 3') are stiffly upright little evergreens with long, flat leaves and spiky stems decorated in fall and winter with fat red berries. Alexandrian laurel is the more graceful of the two, with the wispy look of bamboo. Indeed, it partners delightfully with heavenly bamboo (*Nandina domestica*; Zone 7; 3'–6'), a feathery little shrub with marvelous fall and winter leaf color, creamy or shell-pink flowers, and small red berries tucked among its slim, tapered leaves. Once established, this lacy-looking confection will compete admirably with tree roots and take dry soils in stride. Alexandrian laurel and nandina both fruit best when grown in small colonies in light or broken shade.

Skimmias also need company because the sexes are on separate plants, and females need a male nearby in order to bear fruit. *Skimmia japonica* (Zone 7; 2' to 5') offers a multitude of named forms. All are compact evergreens with leathery, creased foliage. Their rosy buds open into small, fragrant clusters of white flowers that are followed by shiny berries, which may be red, black or white.

Many daphnes are happiest in shade, and certain of them tolerate summer-dry soils. Laurel spurge (*Daphne laureola*; Zone 7; to 4') seeds itself into woodlands and shaded meadow verges, filling the air with piercingly sweet perfume from late winter into spring. Leggy and modestly good looking, this evergreen needs firm support from companions such as small rhododendrons or mountain laurels. *Daphne odora* 'Aureomarginata' (Zone 7; 4'–8'), with leaves edged in pale gold, is slightly hardier than the plain form and blooms generously in shady sites with dry, open-textured soils.

Though nearly always recommended for sunny spots, certain pyracanthas will grow and flower abundantly in dry shade. In my garden, yellow-berried *P.* 'Gold Rush' thrives in extremely dry soil, sandwiched between an elderly weeping birch and a lusty holly.

Mountain laurels are notably accepting of seasonally dry soils and shady sites. Standard forms are mannerly, upright shrubs that open clusters of white or pale pink goblet-shaped flowers from baroquely pleated buds. *Kalmia latifolia* 'Shooting Star' (Zone 4; 4'–6'), has more open, informal white flowers that appear a bit later than usual. New colors include 'Sarah' (to 5'), with rosy blossoms above bronzed new foliage, and 'Bullseye' (to 8'), with a strikingly striped burgundy eye zone.

In small spaces dwarf evergreens are invaluable, particularly those with multiple gifts. Dwarf sweet box (*Sarcococca hookeriana* var. *humilis*; Zone 6; to 18") runs quietly between bigger companions, sending up short stems decked with glossy, tapered leaves and,

Lamiastrum galeobdolon   *Polygonatum odoratum* 'Variegatum'

5; 6'–8') and their hybrids, also bloom prolifically in light or partial shade, and established plants are not at all disturbed by summer drought. Their splendid foliage remains lovely long after the fleeting flowers have faded.

Perennials

A surprising number of perennials will mingle with these shrubs in dry, shady borders and increase happily. Many hostas and ferns grow well in such conditions, including the majestic partnership of *Hosta* 'Krossa Regal' (Zone 3; to 3'), dapper in blue-gray seersucker and the golden-scaled male fern *Dryopteris cristata* 'The King' (Zone 4; to 4'), which has ornately tassled frond tips.

Wood spurges also enjoy these conditions, sowing themselves into their preferred positions at the base of trees and shrubs. Ruddy-leaved *Euphorbia amygdaloides* 'Purpurea' (Zone 5; to 2') performs best when not overcrowded and can be prone to powdery mildew in very dry settings. Robb's spurge, (*E. a.* var. *robbiae*; Zone 5; to 3') is a vigorous creeper whose wandering ways are kept nicely in check by dry soils and deep shade, where its lustrous leaves and chartreuse inflorescences are welcome. A thicketing Himalayan, *E. griffithii* (Zone 5; to 4'), grows and flowers well in deep shade, but cultivars such as the hot red 'Fireglow' and the brick-red 'Dixter' color better in partial sun.

Woodland wildflowers such as bleeding hearts and foxgloves make themselves thoroughly at home in dry shade. The vigorous hybrid *Dicentra* 'Luxuriant' (Zone 3; 1') offers slate-blue, lacy foliage and a long succession of warm red flowers. Common *D. spectabilis* (Zone 3; to 3') won't bloom all summer but will hold its leaves far longer in shade than in sun. Tall foxgloves (*Digitalis purpurea*; Zone 4; 3'–6') rise like belled jester's wands, tipped in cream, pink or soft purple. 'Sutton's Apricot' self-sows reliably in peachy patches,

in winter, tufts of whiskery ivory flowers that exude a sumptuous scent of honey and vanilla. *Leucothoe axillaris* (Zone 6; 3'–4') and *L. fontanesiana* (Zone 5; to 4') are southeastern natives with elegantly arching branches and shiny foliage that colors hotly in autumn and winter; new spring growth is a coppery red. Their cascading shape contrasts wonderfully with the stiff fans and splayed seedpods of *Iris foetidissima* (Zone 6; to 2').

Deciduous hydrangeas provide frothy mounds of long-lasting bloom in almost any color you like, from white, cream or ivory through pink, lavender and mauve, to rose, ruby, sky blue and turquoise, all enriched by vinaceous purples. Young plants need supplemental water for a few seasons, but mature specimens are indestructible dowagers of the dry, shady garden. Tree peonies, notably *Paeonia delavayi* (Zone 5; to 4') and *delavayi* var. *lutea* (Zone

groundcovers for DRY SHADE

Good groundcovers for these difficult conditions include many of the dead nettles, particularly forms of *Lamium maculatum* (Zone 3; 8"). 'White Nancy', 'Beacon Silver', and 'Cannon's Gold' are all strong performers in dry shade. A close cousin, yellow archangel (*Lamiastrum galeobdolon*; Zone 4; 1'), is a weedy sprawler in its typical form, but the selection 'Hermann's Pride' is a glorious carpeter, with narrow, dark leaves abundantly splashed with metallic silver and bearing masses of soft yellow flowers over a long season. Bugleweeds are also good candidates, notably forms of *Ajuga reptans* (Zone 3; 3" to 10"). The darker of these tend to be slow spreaders in dry soils, but given time they pour into luxuriant carpets of burgundy, purple or near black. Spinach ajuga (*A. r.* 'Metallica Crispa') has crinkled, molasses-colored leaves while 'Atropurpurea' is bronzed burgundy. Both bear deep blue flowers. Paler 'Tricolor' is washed with cream and rose and sage while 'Silver Carpet' is fine-textured and suitably pewtery.

provided it is kept well away from the purple wildlings, and so too will the gentle 'Sutton's Giant Primrose'.

All sorts of hardy geraniums work their way into dry shade. Mourning widow (*Geranium phaeum*; Zone 4; to 3') spreads in enormous clumps under a birch tree in my garden. Most of the clumps are variegated like their mother (*G. p.* 'Variegata'), with dim, purple-black flowers. As the shade lightens, they are joined by blue and white forms of meadow geranium (*G. pratense*; Zone 5; to 4'), long bloomers that repeat well when kept from setting their copious seed. At ground level, *G. macrorrhizum* (Zone 4; 1') in many forms canters across the ground, its large, furry leaves punctuated for much of the summer by pink or rosy flowers.

Where summers are hotter, plants that fade fast in full sun may linger longer in shade, however dry. In North Carolina, garden designer Edith Eddleman grows silver-edged Solomon's seal (*Polygonatum odoratum* var. *pluriforum* 'Variegatum'; Zone 4; to 2.5') on a sandy bank under an oak tree, and again smack against the base of a *Magnolia grandiflora*. Many little bulbs flourish in dry shade for her, notably fall-blooming *Crocus goulimyi* (Zone 3; 3") and the marbled *Cyclamen hederifolium* (Zone 5; 5"), both of which demand a dry dormant period in the summer. Bluebells of several kinds and ground orchids, including a number of hybrid bletillas, also persist and bloom well in dry shade.

Eddleman's extensive collection of ivies does well on the same arid, shady bank, where their curly leaves and wavy margins eddy and flow, suggesting the rippling movement of water. The ivy leaves col-

Euphorbia amygdaloides 'Purpurea'

lect humus over time, and hellebores self-sow in the pockets of richer soil, as does *Arum italicum* (Zone 5; 18") and the native green dragon, *Arisaema dracontium* (Zone 4; 2'). Of the epimediums, she finds that *E. ×versicolor* 'Sulphureum' (Zone 5; to 15") is the best of this shade-loving genus for really dry situations where it is often joined by self-sown blue mistflower (*Eupatorium coelestinum*; Zone 5; 6").

Grasses

Grasses that enjoy dry shade include evergreen, cream-striped *Luzula maxima* 'Marginata' (now known as *L. sylvatica* 'Marginata'; Zone 6; 18"), which quickly builds into large and handsome tussocks, and sea oats (*Chasmanthium latifolium*; Zone 3; 3'–5'). Bowles' golden grass (*Milium effusum* 'Aureum'; Zones 6–9; 18") is a fitful perennial that self-sows abundantly in dry shade where its golden leaves and airy seed heads are turned to gilded aureoles by slanting sun rays.

soil PREPARATION

Because any dry, relatively dark setting is a challenging one, it makes sense to give those carefully chosen plants the best possible start. This means amending the existing soil, which is often dusty and exhausted. To improve both tilth and drainage, add copious quantities of humus. My own favorite combination is a blend of compost and aged or pit-washed dairy manure. Lay it down thickly, adding generous amounts of chopped or pelletized alfalfa (a common goat food), which causes a synergistic release of nitrogen when combined with manures. If the soil is not desperately poor, you can dig in this mixture before planting. Otherwise, remove the soil to a depth of 1' (or more, if you are young and strong or wealthy enough to pay somebody else to do this part). Replace it with fresh topsoil, not neglecting the amendments outlined above. Heavy, clay-based soils will benefit from the addition of coarse builder's sand (the kind used on roads in winter, not sandbox stuff, which turns clay into adobe) to increase drainage. An annual mulch of compost and aged manure will keep your renewed soil in good heart. This may seem a lot of effort, but the result is worth it all, for your dry, difficult site will be transformed into a living garden that remains attractive all through the year.

FROM DROUGHT TO DELUGE

choosing a palette of plants that thrive despite climatic extremes

by LAUREN SPRINGER

After gardening in Colorado for a dozen years, I thought I could handle any climatic insult. There is a reason why meteorologists consider this state a mecca; as the local adage goes, if you don't like the weather, wait five minutes.

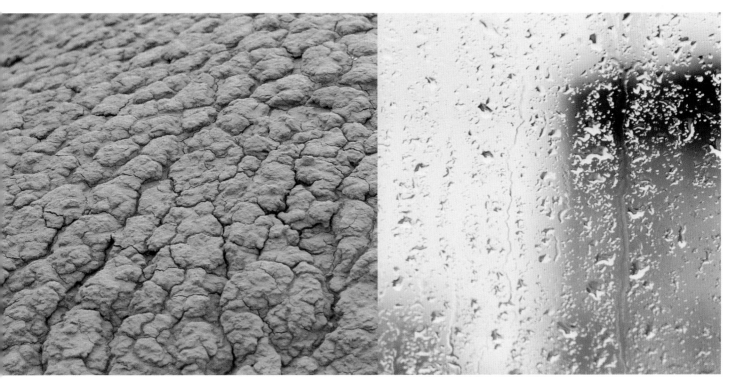

In the relatively short time I've lived here, I've endured several summers with a record-breaking number of days above 90°F, winds well over 100 miles per hour, two winters that saw the mercury dip to 30 below, three garden-wrecking hailstorms, April and October snows of over 3' each, and, on one Halloween, a temperature drop of 70° in 24 hours.

Yet nothing prepared me for the most recent weather patterns, or for the peculiarities of my present site. In 1999, 14" of rain fell between April and June, more than we often see in an entire year. Many dryland plants — bearded iris, penstemon, buckwheat — bloomed like never before and then rotted. The courtyard garden, where I planted more traditional, irrigated fare, was under 1" of water for well over a month. Algae covered the flagstone path to the house, as the hillside above seeped water until mid-July. The creek in the canyon washed out the road and two bridges, stranding several families. Cliffs wept waterfalls for weeks; sheets of wildflowers burst from the surreally green grassland.

Then it all dried up. For two and a half years and running,

northern Colorado has been in a severe drought. On my site we measured 9" of moisture in 2000, and just shy of 7" in 2001. Our once-productive well ran dry the past two summers, a misery incomprehensible to suburbanites and city dwellers who can usually run for the hose. In the once-moist courtyard, I have watched most of the trees, shrubs and perennials succumb. Many bulb species have fared well, which is to be expected, since their life cycle evolved to deal with such extremes. Rising from the ashes of meteorological devastation is another group of plants that thrived in the muck of the flood and have mastered the parched clay — a category of plants never found in gardening books. I have learned about them the hard way, by trial and error, and am now filling the many gaps with more of these adaptable grasses and perennials. After all the wheelbarrows of dead and dying plants have been dragged from the courtyard, there's still hope. A new garden is growing, soon to be a resplendent steppe planting of the toughest of the tough.

Although this kind of gardening is new to me, and there is very little information available, certain patterns are already emerging.

Most obvious is their provenance — mainly prairie and steppe regions that experience intense seasonal variation in moisture, from deluge to drought, on a regular basis. Also, plants adapted to clay soils seem better able to thrive in both extremes, perhaps because a wet clay soil is a far cry from a wet sandy soil, which is rarely if ever truly saturated and anaerobic. A closer look also reveals that certain genera and even families have an inborn adaptability. *Eryngium*, *Paeonia*, and *Euphorbia* are winners, and the legumes are well represented by *Baptisia*, *Dalea* and *Thermopsis*. Taproots and root systems that are sparse and/or slightly tuberous dominate among the survivors. In a number of instances, the more fibrous-rooted species within the same genus succumbed, while the deeply-probing, thicker rooted species survived; *Nepeta sibirica* and the centaureas are cases in point.

Also, when looking within a genus that is generally a moisture-tolerant one, the species that adapt to drought tend to be those with leathery and/or blue foliage. It should be emphasized that this is true only within genera that tolerate moisture — just having blue or leathery leaves does not qualify a plant as tolerant of both extremes. In fact, most drought-loving plants with these characteristics rotted during the wet period. But a look at the numerous *Amsonia*, *Vernonia*, *Solidago* and *Thalictrum* species that were tried reveals that in all cases the surviving species has distinctively thicker, more leathery or waxy leaves, often with a blue color.

My hope is that most gardeners do not have to concern themselves with such conditions. As a friend once said upon visiting my stunning but challenging site and hearing my tale of woe, "For the good fortune of living in such beauty, you deserve your share of trials and tribulations." There's a reason so much of the West's splendor is unspoiled — it is, for the most part, nonarable, untameable land in an unforgiving climate. The key to gardening here lies in utilizing native plants and those from similar parts of the world, a mantra that applies to gardeners everywhere if we are to create beautiful, thriving, ecologically intelligent gardens.

the toughest OF THE TOUGH

PERENNIALS

Amsonia illustris (other bluestar species were severely stunted by drought)

Baptisia australis

B. minor

Centaurea macrocephala

C. orientalis (other species rotted)

Cephalaria alpina

Clematis integrifolia and its hybrids

Dalea purpurea

Delphinium grandiflorum

D. tatsienense

Eryngium giganteum

E. planum

E. yuccifolium

Euphorbia amygdaloides 'Rubra'

E. polychroma

E. palustris

Hemerocallis

Iris missouriensis

I. orientalis

I. spuria (bearded irises rotted; Siberians were severely stunted by drought)

Knautia macedonica

Limonium gmelinii

Nepeta sibirica 'Souvenir d'André Chaudron' (other nepetas rotted)

Paeonia mlokosewitschii

P. obovata

P. tenuifolia

P. tenuifolia x *lactiflora* hybrids (other peonies suffered from drought)

Parthenium integrifolium

Patrinia scabiosifolia

Potentilla atrosanguinea

P. nepalensis and their hybrids

Ratibida pinnata

Salvia forsskaolii

S. nemorosa

S. pratensis

S. verticillata

Sedum telephium 'Munstead Red' (others rotted)

Silphium laciniatum

Solidago rigida (other goldenrods suffered or died from drought)

Tanacetum parthenium 'Aureum'

Thalictrum flavum subsp. *glaucum*

Thermopsis fabacea

Vernonia missurica (other ironweeds died from drought)

Veronica longifolia 'Blue Giant'

Veronicastrum sibiricum

GRASSES AND SEDGES

Andropogon gerardii

Calamagrostis ×*acutiflora* 'Karl Foerster'

C. brachytricha

Carex grayi

Panicum virgatum

Schizachyrium scoparium

Sesleria autumnalis

S. caerulea

S. heufleriana

Sorghastrum nutans (not 'Sioux Blue' — seed-grown Indian grass is more drought-tolerant)

Sporobolus heterolepis

Stipa calamagrostis

First row, top: *Iris spuria, Ratibida pinnata, Centaurea macrocephala, Thalictrum flavum* subsp. *glaucum.* **Second row:** *Eryngium yuccifolium, Paeonia tenuifolia, Salvia verticillata* 'Purple Rain', *Clematis integrifolia.* **Third row:** *Schizachyrium scoparium, Calamagrostis brachytricha, Sorghastrum nutans, Calamagrostis ×acutiflora* 'Karl Foerster'. **Fourth row:** *Tanacetum parthenium, Potentilla atrosanguinea, Sesleria autumnalis.*

NATIVES FOR THE WATER'S EDGE

a selection of perennials that flourish in wet soils

by CAROL BISHOP MILLER

If you're fortunate enough to have a stream or pond on your premises, chances are you already enjoy some of the dozens of attractive native plants adapted to the wet soil or shallow water at the water's edge.

And with the increasing popularity of preformed plastic or fiberglass pools and artificial water features constructed with synthetic flexible liners, these stalwart marginals or otherwise moisture-loving, born-in-the-U.S.A. perennials are bringing grace and beauty and attracting wildlife to more and more gardens.

Many true marginals seem to have the idea that they are commissioned to take over the world. Take, for example, the primitive, spore-bearing horsetail or scouring rush (*Equisetum hyemale*; USDA Zone 3; to 5'), a strange, otherworldly creature packed with silica and historically used for pot scrubbing. (Hold a lit match beneath a stem and watch the beads of glass form.) With its profusion of slender, jointed, dark green stems, one might select horsetail for a dramatic curtain behind a piece of pond statuary, for it multiplies rapidly, quickly filling in where mass effect is desired. That is to say, it spreads like wildfire in all directions and is the devil to eradicate where not wanted. Horsetail is evergreen (though it may be laid low by slings and arrows of an outrageous winter) and thrives in sun or shade in either shallow water or, once established, most soils. In fact, I've seen it take over a raised bed of desert succulents. But in a small pond, horsetail's racing rhizomes can be corralled in a container.

Another screen or strong vertical accent for the water's edge is the common cattail (*Typha latifolia*; Zone 2; to 10'). Native to practically all of North America, cattail is a routine sight along roadsides, where it colonizes thickly by rhizomes in wet ditches and low,

Orontium aquaticum

marshy ground. In late spring and summer the sleek, swordlike leaves are joined by stiff stalks bearing terminal spikes of densely packed flowers — golden, pollen-dusty, short-lived male flowers on top, a velvety soft, brown cylinder of female flowers beneath. It's estimated that a single spike may produce more than 200,000 seeds, each attached to its own little feathery parachute and crammed together so tightly that the merest pinch will quickly expand to fill one's hand with gossamer fluff.

Cattails flourish in full or part sun in permanently wet ground or shallow water, either stagnant or slow-moving. Indeed, I have found cattails thriving in the most unappetizingly sour muck, and so firmly rooted one would think they were fastened to the very core of the earth by some powerful suction. In a small pond, one might want to confine their antics to a container.

Several species of birds, most notably the red-winged blackbird, nest among cattails, and others use the strong, straplike leaves in nest construction. While the almost microscopic seeds are of little interest to birds, chickadees and others feast on the caterpillars that seek winter shelter inside the fluff-packed seed spikes, and birds have been observed catching food inside the spikes. Bear in mind that the larvae of the cattail mosquito, the leading carrier of eastern equine encephalitis, overwinter attached to the roots and rhizomes of cattails and other aquatic plants. If dragonflies, damselflies, fish or other natural enemies fail to provide control, garden centers offer *Bacillus thuringiensis* var. *israelensis*, a bacterial larvicide, in a slow-release, floating tablet form.

Though far less rambunctious, the wetland irises have similarly imposing swordlike leaves, particularly southern blue flag (*Iris virginica*; Zone 5), selections of which can exceed 6' when grown in shallow water in full sun. The flowers, which appear in midspring, are some 4" across, their lilac-to-hot-purple falls delicately veined and brushed with yellow. Northern blue flag (*I. versicolor*; Zone 3; to 3') blooms at the same time, with lavender to violet flowers, the falls of which are accented with stubby fans of white stripes. Copper iris (*I. fulva*; Zone 3; to 5'), one of some five species and their hybrids collectively termed Louisiana irises, presents

Lysichiton americanus

brick-colored flowers whose outstretched-falls and standards give them a characteristic flat-topped look.

Although most water-loving plants are best transplanted in early spring, when they are raring to grow and the threat of winter rot is far removed, irises are best set out in late summer or early fall to ensure a strong spring showing. If not actually under water, the rhizomes should be mulched to prevent sunburn and subsequent decay. Wetland irises need rich soil and year-round moisture to bloom.

Unlike the flashy, conspicuously flaunted blossoms of the irises, the greenish-yellow aroid flower spikes of sweet flag (*Acorus calamus*; Zone 5; to 6') peek out shyly from among the aromatic swordlike leaves. The leaves, which are boldly striped with cream in the variety 'Variegatus', retain their pleasant, citruslike scent when dried for indoor arrangements. Native to most of the northern hemisphere, sweet flag forms dense clumps in sun or shade in damp soil or shallow water.

Certain less lofty arum family members make showy accents along the water's edge. Like burning candles protruding above the water through waxen, oval, 1'-long leaves, the pointed, sinuously curving floral spikes of golden club or bog torch (*Orontium aquaticum*; Zone 6; to 2'), are reddish at the base, gleaming white in the center and brightly tipped with multitudinous tiny yellow flowers. The spring or early-summer display is most enchanting when reflected in a still, dark pool, but this clump-forming eastern native makes a splash in any shallow water, swift or stagnant.

An equally stunning aroid for a muddy bank or extremely shallow (to 3") water is the western skunk cabbage (*Lysichiton americanus*; Zone 6; to 2' or more). Whereas the ill-scented eastern skunk cabbage (*Symplocarpus foetidus*) is more curious than ornamental, this cousin from the western states (whose own objectionable odor is faint unless the tissue is freshly injured) offers sunshine-yellow spathes in early spring before the enormous, inwardly curling leaves emerge.

With its triangular, tropical-looking leaves, arrowhead, or duck potato (*Sagittaria latifolia*; Zone 3; to 4'), native to most of North America, is easily mistaken for an arum family member, but the crisp white flowers, borne all summer long in stacked whorls of three upon tall stems, reveal its membership in the water plantain family (*Alismataceae*). Arrowhead's stringy roots form numerous potatolike tubers that really do feed waterfowl (as well as beavers and muskrats). Arrowhead colonizes in either shallow water or soggy soil and adapts happily to a small pool or even a pot of mud on a sunny patio.

Of special value because its sleek, elongated, heart-shaped leaves are topped by pale blue to violet spikes of bloom from late spring well into autumn, pickerel weed (*Pontederia cordata*; Zone 5; to 4'; sometimes euphemistically — and less accurately — termed pickerel rush) forms expansive clumps in still, shallow water. This mannerly cousin of the notoriously invasive water hyacinth (*Eichhornia crassipes*) is a nectar source for butterflies and hummingbirds, and mosquito-eating damselflies and dragonflies lay their eggs in the buoyant, air-filled stems. A white-flowering form is available.

At first glance one might take powdery thalia (*Thalia dealbata*; Zone 6) for a canna, for certainly the rubbery, oblong, 3' to 5' leaves, held aloft on long petioles, give a similar impression of tropical corpulence. The purple flowers and fruits, however, borne from late spring into fall, are clustered like grapes atop soaring 10' scapes and the entire plant appears to have been dusted with flour. This rare member of the arrowroot family (*Marantaceae*), occasionally encountered in wet ditches and shallow water from South Carolina westward to Missouri and Texas, adapts complacently to life in a submerged container, where its upward mobility, however, is significantly thwarted.

Hibiscus moscheutos

Acorus calamus 'Variegatus'

Cartha palustris

Among native ferns, cinnamon and royal fern (*Osmunda cinnamomea* and *O. regalis*, respectively) are especially fine to set beside water, where their stately, almost treelike clumps of gracefully arching fronds lend softness and composure to a scene. Both are hardy into Canada and take sun readily as long as their feet are damp. In fact, they are the only ferns of which I am aware that will actually thrive in a few inches of water.

But my favorite fern for such a setting is the southern shield fern (*Thelypteris kunthii*, also listed as *T. normalis*), which, in loose, moist soil, stretches about on creeping rhizomes to make of itself a caressing wave of broad, light green fronds, 3' to 4' high. This fern is hardy to at least Zone 7 and probably, in a sheltered spot with a protective blanket of pine straw or leaf mold, to Zone 6.

Grasses ripple seductively in the wind; have great appeal for wildlife, particularly birds; and combat erosion on stream and pond banks. *Spartina pectinata* 'Aureomarginata' (Zone 4; to 4' or more), a variegated version of the North American cordgrass, with narrow, arching, seemingly sunstruck yellow-edged leaves, turns a penchant for invasiveness into an asset as it spreads thickly about to knit together a fragile bank. Cordgrass is tolerant of brackish or polluted water, too.

Less frisky is the clump-forming tufted hair grass (*Deschampsia caespitosa*; Zone 4; to 4'), whose tufts of sleek, thin leaves are crowned in summer by wispy clouds of minuscule blooms. Native throughout much of the northern hemisphere, this moisture-loving grass does best in partial shade.

Some moisture-loving native perennials are made welcome at the rims of our streams and ponds not for their form or function but simply for the gaiety or glamour of their floral display. What cheerier sight could one behold than that of a host of golden marsh marigolds, gleaming like little suns beside a watery reflection of a clear spring sky? Marsh marigold (*Caltha palustris*; Zone 3), common to pond margins and soggy, sunny meadows from Alaska to Newfoundland and southward through the eastern half of the United States, is actually a member of the buttercup family (*Ranunculaceae*). In spring the mounded mats of glossy, spinach-green, heart-shaped leaves are spattered with 1"- to 2"-wide blossoms whose sepals (rather than petals) are of a brilliant, highly polished yellow.

Only once (in southern Georgia) have I encountered the flamboyant red rose mallow (*Hibiscus coccineus*; Zone 7; to 8') in the wild, but its equally statuesque cousin the swamp rose mallow (*H. moscheutos*; Zone 5) is a familiar sight in marshes and along lake shores throughout the eastern half of the country. Both bloom all summer. *Hibiscus coccineus* sports flaring, saucer-size crimson flowers; the leaves are palmately divided into narrow segments. The broad blossoms of *H. moscheutos* resemble those of an okra plant and range from cream to rose, usually featuring a dark maroon center. The leaves are variable in outline. Either plant is at home in moist soil or shallow water, fresh or brackish, in full sun.

If one were inclined to project personalities onto plants, one might describe the cardinal flower (*Lobelia cardinalis*; Zone 4; to 4') as volatile — exciting to be sure, but unreliable. To glimpse its reddest of-red terminal racemes against the cool green of a shaded bank or reflected in dark water is indeed a thrill, but this showy eastern native — which blooms in midsummer to early fall — can be discouragingly elusive, persisting where it's happy, but vanishing posthaste where it's not.

The great blue lobelia (*L. siphilitica*; Zone 4; to 3'), on the other hand, is calm and dependable, blooming earlier and longer than cardinal flower and seeding itself about with welcome abandon into broad colonies. Both species inhabit streamsides, wet ditches and damp meadows, and cardinal flower is sometimes observed growing in several inches of water.

White-flowering forms of both plants are available, and in the case of *L. cardinalis*, pink. Then there is *L. ×gerardii*, a vigorous (to 5') purple-flowering cross between *L. cardinalis* and *L. siphilitica*. In recent years, North Carolina nurseryman Thurman Maness has released a host of hardy lobelia hybrids with flowers in a range of glowing colors. Among the most outstanding are 'Rose Beacon' in rosy pink; 'Ruby Slippers' in deep crimson, and 'La Fresco' in muted plum.

Lobelias are all the more striking when accompanied by spider lily (*Hymenocallis caroliniana*; Zone 5; to 2'), an eastern native amaryllid that erupts in mid- to late summer with a starburst of bewitching, lilylike white flowers. This species thrives in wet (not submerged) soil in sun or shade.

If you have room, save a place at water's edge for a clump of swamp, or narrow-leaved, sunflower (*Helianthus angustifolius*; Zone 6; to 7'). With slender, 8" leaves that turn under at the edges, narrow-leaved sunflower has uncommonly handsome foliage for the genus. In late summer or early autumn this sun- and moisture-loving roadside native becomes a dazzling jumble of 2"- to 3"-wide, dark-eyed yellow daisies. Pruning back in early summer controls height and promotes branching.

Picture this brilliant daisy cavorting about an opalescent pond amid the frizzy, purple-red florets of ironweed (*Vernonia* spp.), pinkish puffs of joe-pye weed (*Eupatorium maculatum*) and a gauzy cloud of blue mistflower (*Eupatorium coelestinum*). Surely Monet would approve.

Pontederia cordata

Osmunda regalis

SOME LIKE IT WET

many perennials will thrive in boggy conditions

by JEFF COX

If you have a spot where your shoes always get muddy and skunk

cabbage grows thick and lush, you're in luck. You have a bog.

Let the skunk cabbage (*Symplocarpus foetidus*) grow. It's the first harbinger of spring, and its flame-shaped spathes, containing flower-covered spadices, produce enough heat to warm holes through the snow. The spathes are a promising sight in late winter, and are

If you have a piece of damp ground, don't despair. As Beth Chatto has demonstrated at her garden in Essex Market, England, moisture-loving perennials — particularly those with distinctive foliage — can create brilliant effects.

a bog OF ONE'S OWN

If you want to grow moisture-loving plants but lack the right conditions, you can create a boggy spot. Lay down a 30-mil pond liner in a shallow hole (the overall dimensions should match your ambition, but the hole itself should be about 8" to 12" deep). Bring the liner to ground level and drape it out about 6" onto the soil surface. Where it bunches, just fold it flat. With a utility knife, make 8"-long slits every 3' or 4' in every direction in the bottom. Don't pull the slits apart. Fill your bog with good, humusy soil, then cover the pond liner at the soil surface with soil and stones. Water your new bog to the saturation point. Water will slowly leak out through the slits in the bottom, but conditions will remain constantly moist for weeks. If the soil seems dry, simply run the hose on it until it's wet again. Artificial bogs are best placed out of the way of foot traffic, unless you like muddy shoes.

followed by big, decorative, cabbagelike leaves in spring and summer.

Why not enhance and prolong the display by taking advantage of the many gorgeous perennials that enjoy a boggy spot? With their varied flora, including aquatics, small woody plants and grasses, bogs are among the most biologically diverse places on anyone's property; adding the beauty of perennials simply enriches the mix.

A bog isn't one narrowly definable kind of place, but rather a continuum of wet places. At one extreme is shallow standing water, hosting watercress, horsetail, water arum and pickerel weed. Above-water zones range from continually wet marshes to boggy meadows that can dry out in periods of summer drought. Some perennials will thrive in continually wet marshes, but most of those that tolerate wet feet prefer the slightly better-drained boggy meadow.

Boggy places can occur naturally for several reasons. First, a piece of land may be poorly drained and contain a shallow basin where rainwater collects. Second, the bog may mark a transitional area between a pond or stream and drier land. Third, the bog may be caused by springs coming to the surface. The last two kinds of bog are by far the most common.

Getting Through

If your bog is a large one, chances are you're going to want some means of access through it, the better to appreciate the plants. A path through a natural bog, however, requires some planning. Water moves slowly through natural bogs, finding an outlet somewhere, even if it's down through the soil. If you construct a raised path, you run the risk of damming up the

Some grasses and grasslike plants are too invasive for the carefully planted bog garden. Avoid the common reed (*Phragmites australis*) and its cultivars, for they are horribly invasive on newly turned wet soil, spreading by strong rhizomes, much like bamboo. Reed canary grass (*Phalaris arundinacea*) is a European import that has become a major threat to marshlands in the northern United States, where it chokes out native species. Cattails (*Typha* spp.) can also be aggressive colonizers of marshes. The tall species, *T. angustifolia* and *T. latifolia*, will quickly take over your bog and elbow out other species. You can safely get away with the miniature cattail, *T. minima*, though, which grows to about 2.5' tall and is much better behaved than its larger cousins. One plant to avoid for sure is purple loosestrife (*Lythrum salicaria*), which is overwhelming native species throughout the wet areas of the northern states. In fact, it's against the law to plant it in some places. Despite its beauty, it's a first-class pest.

water flow on one side or the other of the path, where it will turn stagnant (and stinky) and attract mosquitoes.

The solution is to construct a small bridge every 10' to 12', so that water can flow underneath and find its escape. A bridge can be as simple as a sturdy plank laid over a 3'-wide break in the path, supported by stones flat enough to keep footing secure. Or it can be a Japanese footbridge — a simple but attractive affair. Bridges make excellent viewing points, since they funnel traffic along a specific route. Walk around your bog to see if there are any other natural viewing points. You might want to site a bench there.

Design Considerations

At my former house in Pennsylvania, my back deck looked out over a marshy area about 100' × 60' where two springs came to the surface. From the deck down to the ground was at least 10', so close to the deck I planted tall perennials — specifically queen of the prairie (*Filipendula rubra* 'Venusta') and *Eupatorium* 'Gateway'. The filipendula is a stunning sight when it blooms from mid-June through July, opening fluffy, cotton-candy plumes of rich rose pink on 4' to 7' stems. 'Gateway' can reach 6', with puffy heads of reddish purple to mauve florets from August to October. Looking down onto these marsh plants, I had a continual display of bloom from June through October.

Natural viewing points in most bog gardens, however, are at eye level. As you survey your boggy area, think about planting the perennials to form tiers, with the smallest plants in front and the largest in back, so that each one is easily seen. Vary the pattern, however, just as you would in an ordinary border, by mixing in large clumps of grasses, sedges or other foliage plants.

Where there is shallow standing water, the three-way sedge (*Dulichium arundi-*

In a brilliant late-spring scene at Beth Chatto's garden, sedges, forget-me-nots and orange *Euphorbia griffithii* set off the unfurling lime-green croziers of ostrich fern (*Matteuccia struthiopteris*).

naceum) is a possibility, along with the clumps of shaggy tussock grass (*Carex stricta*), which likes the same conditions as skunk cabbage. Another exceptionally pretty sedge is Bowles' golden sedge (*Carex elata* 'Aurea'), which grows into a fountain of slender golden leaves by midsummer and holds its shape and color until fall. The cloudlike masses of fine-flowering tufted hair grass (*Deschampsia cespitosa*) make beautiful companions to larger-leaved perennials, and are especially effective against a background of dark conifers. Variegated manna grass (*Glyceria maxima* var. *variegata*) mixes well with darker-leaved bog plants like rodgersias. The graceful, upright stems of the common rush (*Juncus effusus*) belong in the bog garden, too.

Among other foliage plants for the bog garden, one would think hostas appropriate, since they like consistently moist soil, but they thrive only where drainage is good. The solution is to plant them upslope a bit from the real boggy areas. Ferns are a natural choice for damp soils. Cinnamon fern (*Osmunda cinnamomea*) and shield fern (*Polystichum braunii*) like the same moist yet well-drained conditions as hostas. For constantly wet, marshy areas, consider lady fern (*Athyrium filix-femina*), crested wood fern (*Dryopteris cristata*) and the glorious royal fern (*Osmunda regalis*), which grows up to 6' tall and can anchor the back of a boggy perennial border as well as — or better than — any other plant.

In cold areas, cleanup is often best carried out during freezing weather; by that point, deciduous shrubs will have shed their leaves, herbaceous plants will have died down, and the ice underfoot will keep your feet from getting muddy. Unless, of course, you like galumphing through the mud of your gorgeous bog garden, like a kid delirious with the joy of it all.

how to make a
JAPANESE PLANK FOOTBRIDGE

This simple bridge is easy to make from wood sold for post-and-rail fencing. The 6"- to 8"-diameter uprights should be set deep enough in the soil to be stable, but also so that one pair of holes is 12" to 18" above the soil (or water) level. The spacing between each pair of posts should be great enough to allow for a pair of 2×10 planks to fit between them. The crosspieces can be fashioned from lengths of round rail, although a new tenon will have to be cut by hand on one end of each crosspiece once the rail has been cut to length. To ensure that the crosspieces don't slip out of the holes in the posts, drive a heavy nail through each post into the tenon. Lay out the pair of planks and secure them to the crosspieces with nails so that they don't slip apart.

Polemonium reptans

Filipendula rubra 'Venusta'

Dodecatheon jeffreyi

Matteuccia struthiopteris

Lilium canadense

A SELECTION OF MOISTURE-LOVING PERENNIALS

NAME	USDA HARDINESS ZONE
TWO FEET OR LESS	
Astilbe chinensis var. *pumila*	4–9
Caltha palustris/marsh marigold	3–9
Dodecatheon jeffreyi/shooting star	5–9
Doronicum columnae/leopard's bane	4–9
Gentiana septemfida var. *lagodechiana*	4–9
Geum rivale/water avens	3–8
Liriope spicata/creeping lilyturf	5–9
Myosotis scorpioides var. *semperflorens*/forget-me-not	3–9
Polemonium reptans/Jacob's ladder	3–9
Trillium grandiflorum/white trillium	3–8
TWO TO THREE FEET	
Aquilegia longissima/yellow columbine	3–9
Chelone lyonii/turtlehead	4–9
Dicentra spectabilis/bleeding heart	3–9
Iris ensata/Japanese iris	5–9
Liatris spicata/blazing star	3–10
Lobelia cardinalis/cardinal flower	2–8
Platycodon grandiflorus/balloon flower	3–9
Thalictrum aquilegiifolium/meadow rue	5–9
THREE TO FOUR FEET	
Ligularia dentata 'Desdemona'	4–9
Lilium canadense/meadow lily	4–8
Phlox carolina	4–9
Rudbeckia 'Goldquelle'/coneflower	3–9
Trollius chinensis 'Golden Queen'/globeflower	4–7
FOUR FEET OR MORE	
Aruncus dioicus/goatsbeard	4–9
Cardiocrinum giganteum	5–8
Cimicifuga actaea racemosa/black cohosh	3–9
Eupatorium 'Gateway'/joe-pye weed	4–7
Filipendula rubra 'Venusta'/queen of the prairie	3–9
Hibiscus moscheutos 'Lord Baltimore'/rose mallow	5–9
Thalictrum rochebruneanum/meadow rue	4–9
Veronicastrum virginicum 'Album'/white culver's root	3–9

Bright rose-pink flower spikes to 12" in August–September. Semishade.

Opens clusters of yellow flowers on 12" to 18" stems mid-April–June. Semishade.

Likes wet conditions in late winter and spring; bears distinctive blossoms on 1' or 2' stalks in June, followed by quick dormancy. Semishade.

Toothed leaves send up 1'-tall flower stalks early May–June, topped with bright yellow daisies; disappears by late summer. Full sun–semishade.

Easier to grow than most gentians; bears blue flowers July–August on trailing stems up to 1' tall. Full sun to semishade.

Produces small, drooping purple and orange-pink flowers late May–mid-July on 18" stems. Semishade.

Makes fine, 8"-tall, grasslike patches of foliage with lilac to white flowers late in season. Semishade.

Grows 6" to 10" tall; continues to open tiny bright blue flowers May–frost. Full sun to semishade.

Grows to just 1' tall; makes clumps of fine-looking foliage and light blue flowers. April–July. Semishade.

Makes a low-growing trio of pointed leaves that produce a stem to 1' or more tall with a single white flower on top, late April–May. Full shade.

A beautiful, pale yellow columbine that flowers June–August; spurs are 4" to 6" long on a 2' plant. Full sun.

This swamp denizen produces 2' to 3' stems topped with short spikes of hooded pink flowers August–mid-September. Full–semishade.

One of the prettiest perennials, with heart-shaped pink and white blossoms below arching 2' stems May–June. Semishade.

Flat, beardless flowers appear July–August and come in most colors except pink, surmounting 2' swordlike leaves. Full sun.

In July–September sends up 3' wands of bright rose-purple florets that open from the top down. Plant where winter drainage is good. Full sun.

Opens 30" spikes of intense scarlet flowers late July–September. Likes marshy soil. Full sun–semishade.

Should be more widely planted. In June–July produces many closed-ended flowers on 3' stems that open into flat-faced, lilac stars. Full sun.

Forms an open, 3' structure of columbine-like leaves and puffy flowers May–July in light violet to pink. Self-sows vigorously. Semishade.

Bears large, spotted leaves and sends up 3' stems of bright orange daisies with brown centers. Semishade.

Sports bright orange to red nodding flowers on sturdy 3' to 5' stems in late June to August. Semishade.

In June–July opens clusters of typical phlox flowers in pink, purple or white on 3' to 4' stems. Full sun.

Typically grows 3' to 4' tall, with clusters of metallic yellow daisies atop the stems August–September. Full sun.

Sends up sturdy stems to about 3' May–June, topping them with pretty, bowl-shaped, double flowers. Semishade.

Creamy white plumes rise above ferny foliage and reach 4' to 6' in June–July. Male plants have showier but shorter-lived flowers. Semishade.

One of the most magnificent of flowering perennials, with stalks towering to 10' in midsummer crowned with tubular white lilies. Semishade.

Forms a basal clump of finely divided leaflets; in early July–August produces wands of creamy white florets from 6' to 7'. Semishade.

Makes a dazzling display of rounded, pinkish lilac flower heads to 5' to 6' in August–October. Reddish stems need no staking. Full sun–semishade.

Tops its long, sturdy, 6' stems with shaggy, puffy, rose-pink plumes in June. An outstanding plant to mix with joe-pye weed. Full sun–semishade.

The 4' to 6' stems never need staking; opens huge, 7", brightly colored rose-red blossoms July–October. Looks decidedly tropical. Full sun.

A majestic perennial up to 8' tall that produces tiny lavender-purple flowers along the top third of its tall stems July–September. Semishade.

Looks like a large (5' to 6') veronica, with tall spikes of small florets in a dazzling display early August–late September. Full sun.

WITHIN THE WOODLAND

the art and science of growing wildflowers in the shade

by WILLIAM CULLINA

Over half of North America would be covered by some kind of forest if left to its own devices, but not all forests offer the same growing conditions for gardening.

Deciduous trees like maples, ashes, tulip trees and many oaks allow much of the sun's energy to pass through to the ground during winter and early spring, and the wildflowers in these forests respond with a frenetic burst of activity before the trees leaf out. Evergreens — mostly conifers like spruce, pine and fir, which dominate forests in much of Canada, the mountainous and maritime West and some of the South — are another matter. Since these trees do not lose their leaves in winter, the pace of life in the herbaceous layer is more subdued in spring. Many of the wildflowers, such as bunchberry, are evergreen as well, and most are adapted to the cool, acid soils that form under needle-bearing trees. It is important to take into account the type of trees you have while planning your garden. If maples, ashes, basswoods, tulip trees and beeches predominate, incorporate spring ephemerals that do much of their growth and bloom in early spring. If your trees are mainly evergreen, choose wildflowers that are adapted to cool, acid soils and a slower pace of life. If oaks and hickories form your canopy, a mix of the two should work well.

Even so, remember that even a single tree takes up an enormous amount of space, light and water, and that its roots can spread out 50' or more in all directions. Gardening in these conditions can only be done on the tree's terms. A successful woodland garden must be responsive to the needs and rhythms of the trees, but provide just enough light, good soil and water for the wildflowers to thrive.

Letting in Light

Although shade is a given in woodland gardening, it is a difficult thing to quantify. While sun is sun, shade can be anything from the light shadow of a veil to the darkness of a closet. When planning a woodland garden, I like to aim for dappled shade, where the canopy is thin enough to allow sparkles of sunlight to dance across the forest floor. Limb your trees up as high as you can with a pole pruner, or if an arborist is available remove the lower half of the branches that line the trunk. If your woods are dense with young trees or thick conifers, thin out a quarter of the weakest trees to leave gaps in the canopy. (You should have to squint when looking up on a sunny day.) Understory trees and shrubs add depth to the woodland garden, but use them sparingly — not much can grow underneath the double-layered shade of the woody understory. These larger plants are best grouped or scattered lightly through the woods with gaps for herbaceous plants.

Building Good Soil

Woodland soils grow up, not down. The slow deposition of leaves and wood adds organic matter that fuels decomposition, recycles nutrients and builds up topsoil. The topsoil in many forests (with the exception of those where water has deposited sediments in the past) is fairly shallow, and tree roots do their best to occupy every inch of it. In order to provide space for wildflowers, you will likely have to build the soil up. Quite simply, the deeper your topsoil, the better will be both the quality and quantity of wildflowers. The easiest way to do this is to apply a yearly layer of organic mulch such as shredded leaves, bark or aged wood chips — either in the fall or early spring. Adding a few inches of this material (beyond what the trees would supply naturally) will tip the balance, building up in a few years what would otherwise take decades. Layers of decomposing material have the further benefit of feeding beneficial fungi and providing perfect seedbeds for slow-to-germinate plants like trilliums and orchids.

In general, woodland plants are not heavy feeders, and once the soil is healthy enough, no additional fertilizer is necessary. Until that point is reached, however, a light dressing of a balanced organic fertilizer will help immensely. Apply the fertilizer in spring just as the understory begins to emerge — that way, smaller plants can take up what they need before the trees become active.

Providing Water

Fifty years ago, water restrictions and concerns about pollution were pretty much nonexistent. Today, however, we're much more conscious of what spills out of the hose. When we design new gardens, it makes sense to match the plants to the site, selecting plants that can handle summer drought when necessary. Fortunately, many woodland wild-flowers are active mainly in the spring, so summer dry spells and even an occasional drought will not kill them.

The Different Kinds of Woodland Plants

Woodland gardens put forth a feverish burst of energy in spring. By the summer solstice, though, the garden has transformed into a thousand shades of green, where texture replaces color as the dominant element of design. When planting a woodland garden, therefore, try to follow this rhythm. Plan for and celebrate the early burst of color that evolves gradually into a predominately textural garden in summer — a place of calm, cool shelter from the heat, punctuated by occasional bloom.

Many of the most colorful woodland wildflowers are spring ephemerals, plants that make their above ground growth early and then retreat underground as the tree canopy fills out and the temperature climbs. Ephemerals provide a quick burst of color when we need it most and require no upkeep in the summer, but they leave gaping holes if used to excess. The most successful woodland gardens use these early players as the first act, relying on longer-lasting wildflowers, ferns and woody plants to fill in after they have left the stage. I call this cohabitational planting, and it is a technique that mirrors closely what happens naturally on the forest floor. Aim for a mix of ephemerals for early-season drama, some specimens like trilliums and orchids for a mid-season epiphany and enduring structural plants such as ferns that will provide interest into the fall.

All the plants mentioned below have been reliably hardy for us in USDA Zone 5, and most are hardy well into Zones 3 and 4. I have tried to pick plants that will perform well over most of the forested parts of the United States and southern Canada.

Ephemerals

The yellow trout lily (*Erythronium americanum*) was a familiar sight in forests near my home growing up, with its ground-hugging leaves mottled in gray and brown like the side of a brook trout. This species can be frustrating in

Previous page: When planting a woodland garden, the most satisfying results come from using a combination of early-blooming ephemerals; mid-season specimen plants such as trilliums and orchids; and ferns, groundcover plants, and shrubs for long-term interest. **Above, clockwise from upper left:** Red trillium (*T. erectum*); bunchberry (*Cornus canadensis*); double bloodroot (*Sanguinaria canadensis* f. *multiplex*); celandine poppy (*Stylophorum diphyllum*) and creeping phlox (*P. stolonifera*); *Hepatica americana*; Dutchman's breeches (*Dicentra cucullaria*).

the garden, producing mats of leaves but very few flowers. A bit of fertilizer in the spring (try one formulated for bulbs) and a bright spot will encourage heavier bloom. The western mountains are blessed with a number of larger species that have freely hybridized in cultivation, producing some outstanding garden plants. *Erythronium* 'Pagoda' is a readily available and very satisfying plant that, under good conditions, will form temporary clumps of 8" to 12" glossy leaves and flaring, 2" flowers spaced elegantly on tall stems. Another hybrid, 'White Beauty', is smaller, with creamy white trumpets that flair and curl back at the tips. All the trout lilies are excellent ephemeral companions, quickly retiring underground as the trees leaf out.

As the trout lilies are coming into bloom, Dutchman's breeches (*Dicentra cucullaria*) unfurl filigreed foliage that carpets the ground temporarily in soft blue green, punctuated by arching, 6" stems of white flowers that look like upside-down pantaloons. The flowers are effective for about two weeks if the weather remains cool, by which time its close cousin, squirrel corn (*D. canadensis*) takes the stage. Both species spread quickly by seed and cormlets, which can be dug and scattered about after the plants go dormant (just be sure not to disturb them after Labor Day, since they begin to form new shoots for next season that can be easily damaged).

Iris cristata

Woodland Stars

The carpeting spring ephemerals pave the way for the stars of the spring woodland. Many of these, including trilliums, bloodroot, lady's slippers and phlox, are not truly ephemeral because their foliage persists well into summer and fall, but spring is certainly their finest hour. By the time the dog days of summer arrive, they are looking a bit tattered and sleepy, and so I like to think of them as vernal exclamations, accents that don't need to hold their place all season. Two of the first to bloom, often when frosts still trace your windshield, are bloodroot (*Sanguinaria canadensis*) and hepatica (both *H. acutiloba* and *H. americana*). Bloodroot lofts blink-and-you'll-miss-them flowers of radiant white that spring from the unrolling leaves. Its bold foliage is quite attractive for most of the summer, especially if moisture falls regularly. Hepaticas are one of my favorite spring wildflowers — little mounds of many-petaled violet, blue or white flowers. However, after a wet summer, the usually evergreen foliage becomes tattered and disfigured by the black spot fungi that plague many in the buttercup family. Place hepaticas in a spot with good air movement and drainage and they really shine.

Virginia bluebells (*Mertensia virginica*) emerge from the ground as leafy rosettes stained a deep purple that unfold rapidly and flower for about four weeks with ethereal bells of sky blue (or rarely white

woodland wildflowers
THAT CAN TOLERATE MODERATELY DRY SOIL

Anemonella thalictroides (rue anemone)

Aquilegia canadensis (Canada columbine)

Asarum virginicum (Virginia wild ginger)

Chrysogonum virginianum (golden star)

Gaultheria procumbens (wintergreen)

Geranium maculatum (wild geranium)

Hepatica americana (round-lobed hepatica)

Iris cristata (crested iris)

Mertensia virginica (Virginia bluebells)

Podophyllum peltatum (mayapple)

Sanguinaria canadensis (bloodroot)

Smilacina racemosa (false Solomon's seal)

or rose). They mix beautifully with the buttercup-yellow, four-petalled celandine poppy (*Stylophorum diphyllum*) — an equal match in size and vigor. Both species will liberally self-seed if not deadheaded and may eventually crowd out smaller companions.

As these flowers fade from view, the first of the trilliums begin to bloom. Every spring I am bewitched once again by these elegant wildflowers. I have grown many of the species, but here I will focus on the most satisfactory and easy. Showy trillium (*T. grandiflorum*) is the queen of the genus, with full, white flowers up to 3" across that truly light up the woodland. It is a vigorous species that, once settled in, can form sizable clumps, and if you can think in terms of decades, will seed itself around as well.

Cypripedium parvifloram var. *pubescens*

Its counterpart in the Pacific Northwest is *T. ovatum,* with somewhat smaller white flowers. Red trillium (*T. erectum*), with its faintly fetid, burgundy flowers, is equally easy. Catesby's trillium (*T. catesbyi*) is a good choice for heavy clays in the South. There is a large group of trilliums whose sessile (stemless) flowers nestle in a whorl of typically mottled leaves. The foliar patterns of gray, silver, green and burgundy are at least as interesting as the long-lasting flowers, and I wonder if this camouflage evolved to help hide the plants from colorblind but ravenous deer. Three of the easiest and most readily available are whippoorwill (*T. cuneatum*), with burgundy flowers, yellow trillium (*T. luteum*), with lemon-scented blooms and *T. chloropetalum* and its varieties, with flowers in a range of reds and white.

If you choose carefully, it's possible to have a succession of colorful woodland phloxes in bloom for almost two months. Wood phlox (*P. divaricata*) seeds its way agreeably around the trilliums, providing drifts of blue for several weeks as the trilliums reach their peak. Creeping phlox (*P. stolonifera*) follows on the heels of wood phlox, and its evergreen leaves make a passable ground-hugging carpet for the rest of the year. Ozark phlox (*P. pilosa* subsp. *ozarkiana*) is next to bloom, sporting lavender pinwheels on taller stems. Finally, Alabama phlox (*P. pulchra*) rounds out the display, flowering for us well into June. This species prefers a brighter spot on the edge of the woods.

Lady's slipper orchids remain rarities in gardens, mainly because of the high costs involved in their protracted propagation, but advances in laboratory seedling production should make them cheaper and more readily available over the next few years. Nevertheless, they will continue to have an otherworldly aura about them — they seem almost too intricate and complex to be of this time and place. I have tried most of the native species with degrees of success, but the least demanding are the large and small yellow lady's slippers (*Cypripedium parviflorum* var. *pubescens* and *C. parviflorum*) and the spectacular Kentucky lady's slipper (*C. kentuckiense*). They are closely related plants, sending up stems of alternating, pleated leaves, each tipped with a flower or two in spring. These three species bloom sequentially, so you can have orchids in bloom for a solid month in spring.

stopping WILD COLLECTORS

Commercial wild collecting of woodland wildflowers continues to be a serious threat to their long-term survival. When buying wildflowers, especially slow-growing woodlanders like bloodroot, hepaticas, trilliums and lady's slippers (*Cypripedium pubescens*), be suspicious of suppliers that sell inexpensive (less than $5 to $10 each) and/or bareroot plants. If you're in doubt, ask the nursery about the source of the plants and buy them only if you're convinced they're nursery-propagated. Your local native plant society is often a good source for lists of reputable vendors.

Large yellow lady's slipper is the first to open, gracing our gardens for Mother's Day every year. By the end of May its blooms are fading and the smaller but more intensely colored small yellow lady's slipper is reaching its peak. It has a chrome-yellow pouch as big as a quail's egg and chocolate petals, and blooms appear in spikes of two or three, unlike the typically solitary flowers of its larger relative. Around the second week in June, the magnificent Kentucky lady's slipper begins to bloom. Its flowers are the largest in the genus, with a moonlight-yellow pouch as big as a hen's egg and chocolate petals suffused with raspberry. When people spot it in the garden there is a kind of whispered awe, as though a movie star had just entered the room. As long as you grow the yellow-flowered species in dappled shade and a moist but gritty soil, they should thrive and double or even triple in size within a reasonably short time.

Groundcovers

Groundcovers excel in the shade, filling in gaps around larger plants and often remaining evergreen throughout the winter. Two of the aristocrats among native groundcovers are wandflower (*Galax urceolata*) and its cousin, the rare and lovely Oconee bells (*Shortia galacifolia*). Both are slow to establish but well worth the wait, clothing themselves in lustrous, deep green leaves.

If you want elegance but don't have the conditions or patience for galax or shortia, consider our native Allegheny spurge (*Pachysandra procumbens*). It is a more refined plant than its Japanese relative, with larger, gray-green foliage that turns burgundy as autumn sets in. The change to red reveals silver mottling that was masked by the green, a pleasing foil for the bottlebrush spikes of cinnamon-scented blooms in early spring. As the flowers fade, the clumps erupt with a burst of fresh green leaves to carry them through the next year. Set them in 2' apart and they will form a solid carpet in two to three years.

Gardening beneath the trees has its challenges, but if you learn to work with them, carving out a bit of extra space for wildflowers to thrive, the results can be spectacular. There is really no other type of gardening where so many plants — from the smallest mosses and groundcovers to shrubs and trees — can all inhabit the same small patch of earth.

A spectacular mid-spring display of wood phlox (*P. divaricata*) and the rare double form of showy trillium (*T. grandiflorum* 'Flore Pleno'). This kind of lavishness is possible only when the plants receive sufficient light, moisture and nutrients.

FROM THE WOODLANDS OF ASIA

exotic jack-in-the-pulpits, gingers and other shade-loving gems are now gracing American gardens

by JOAN MEANS

By now, it has become a reflex: Need a plant for a shady place? Pop in a hosta, Japan's greatest gift to American gardeners!

There are, however, other options for gardeners who want more variety or who find that among the demure wildflowers of a naturalistic woodland garden, those mounds of highly puckered and variegated hosta foliage look as overdressed as a sequined dress at a church picnic. For some years I've been searching out bold herbaceous perennials to provide structure in my woods when the early "ephemerals" are past their prime. Although European hellebores and American umbrella leaf play their parts, I've discovered that, once again, Japan (along with neighboring regions in eastern Asia) is a major supplier of outstanding foliage plants for shady gardens.

Encouraged by the demands of an increasingly sophisticated gardening public, nurserymen are now offering many Asian woodland plants that once could be found only in the private gardens of collectors. At the same time, they are sponsoring botanical expeditions to look for plants in the wild and often they are taking a busman's holiday and going along, too. The sheer diversity of the exciting shade plants that are being discovered in newly opened regions of China and Korea, but also in the supposedly well-known forests of Japan, is amazing. Already available by mail order are exotic jack-in-the-pulpits; gingers with large, silver-veined leaves and shade-loving peonies.

And it's becoming clear that there's much more to come. When Darrell Probst, a Massachusetts horticulturist and plant breeder, subscribed to an expedition to China a few years ago his return payment included a seed packet of mixed epimediums, woodland plants known in most gardens by only a few European representatives. But among the Chinese seedlings that Probst grew from that single packet, three have recently been confirmed by British authorities as species new to science. The most spectacular of these is a glossy-leaved, 8"-tall groundcover that boasts taller flowering stems each bearing up to 30 large flowers with sepals .5" wide and centered by a maroon cup and maroon spurs. The new epimedium, Probst announced, is to be called *Epimedium epsteinii,* honoring "my friend and mentor" Harold Epstein, an amateur gardener whose acre of woodland outside New York City became home to a world-famous collection of Japanese and Asian plants. Official

Glaucidium palmatum

Glaucidium palmatum

word of the honor to Epstein arrived from British taxonomists only weeks before his death in 1997 at age 94.

It is fitting that, even as new gardenworthy plants are being introduced, Epstein should be recognized for inspiring generations of American gardeners to gain solid experience growing at least some of the woodland flora of eastern Asia. In recent years we have come to understand that these plants may be uniquely suited to life in the humus-rich soil of forested North America — that indeed, they sometimes share a common ancestry with our own native wildflowers, dating to the period before the two continents drifted apart on their tectonic plates.

As is true of our own wildflowers, discovering whether a plant will be cold-hardy or heat-tolerant isn't always a simple matter of matching latitudes. Who, for example, would expect to see a tropical begonia survive winters north of Boston? Yet *Begonia grandis* subsp. *evansiana*, an inhabitant of China south to Malaysia, has flourished in my USDA Zone 6 garden for years. The red-backed leaves are large and succulent like a rex begonia, and are carried on 2' stems topped by pink or white flowers in September. If ever a plant looked out of place in a New England woodland, this is it! Yet each time I try to move it new plants pop up from tiny tubers left in the old location. After seeing how this begonia has spread over a garden on the shore of Italy's Lake Garda, I imagine it could become a nuisance in southern areas where it has a chance to set seed.

No responsible gardener, of course, wants to see his plants jump the garden gate to invade the space of our native flora. Whenever I acquire a new species of suspect habits and hardiness, I keep it isolated for a year or two in a small trial bed or in a pot plunged in a cold frame. Aggressive self-seeders go to the compost heap, while plants of borderline hardiness, such as *Asarum splendens,* remain protected until divisions or cuttings prove able to survive in the open garden. This ginger is one of several newly introduced Asian species, and it is indeed splendid, with 12"-long evergreen leaves mottled in silver and enormous (for an asarum) 2"-wide flowers with white centers. As yet, I haven't found the right microclimate in my woods, but it should do fine in Zone 7.

Drifts of snow cover the ground of my pine-oak copse for much of the winter, so evergreen leaves are less important than they might be in gardens farther south. Nevertheless, if I'm going to give

space to a foliage plant it has to earn its keep all summer without developing slug-riddled leaves or keeling over into an early-August dormancy. Japan's jack-in-the-pulpits meet those criteria and are large enough to have real visual impact. Plant hunter Barry Yinger has introduced several *Arisaema*

Paeonia veitchii

species that I haven't yet tried, but three other jacks get my slightly qualified "thumbs up." The best known of these is *Arisaema sikokianum*, which in May has spectacular purple-black spathes lined in white, centered with a white, knob-shaped "jack." In rich soil, plants may stand more than 2' tall and probably half of all seedlings will have silver streaks highlighting three-part leaves that can span nearly 2'. I find *A. sikokianum* especially effective when grown in large colonies between the pink-budded mounds of *Rhododendron yakushimanum*, a medium-size shrub with a summertime show of new foliage in shimmering silver.

The lesser-known *A. ringens* is slightly larger in all its parts. The broad leaflets look like shiny green vinyl; lurking beneath is a rather sinister green-and-brown-striped flower, fat and curved like a cobra's head. I like it rising above a lake of ground-covering *Primula kisoana*, a stoloniferous Japanese primrose blessed with rather large and hairy heart-shaped leaves that seem impervious to drought, disease and insects.

As for the exquisite *A. candidissimum*, I fell in love with it 20 years ago when I saw it growing in a Zone 4 garden. My love remained unrequited until only recently, when tubers finally became available in the United States. This jack has pale pink spathes almost like calla lilies and three-part foliage in which each leaflet is easily 1' wide and 14" long.

Because it doesn't emerge until late in June, I find this arisaema especially useful planted among ephemeral wildflowers that go dormant early in summer — plants such as the Japanese *Adonis amurensis* which begins pushing up great yellow buttercups between snowstorms in February, elongates its stems clothed in filigreed leaves in April and May, and ends its season in June as a collapsed, yellowing heap.

If there's a problem with most of the other Asian foliage plants in my woods, it's not that they're difficult or require special attention — merely that they have yet to trickle down into the horticultural mainstream and consequently take some determination to track down. As Darrell Probst explains, "No matter how beautiful and easy to grow, plants will remain rare until customers learn to ask nurserymen for them."

Ah, there's the rub! When these plants have common names, they tend not to be English and their Latin monikers aren't always easy to remember, either. For example, there's the plant I bought as *Aceriphyllum rossii*. The maple-shaped, shiny leaves are 10" wide and stand on 9"-tall stems that are preceded in early spring by naked stalks bearing massive panicles of sparkling white flowers. In moist soil the gradually expanding mound of foliage makes an effective foreground accent among smaller plants such as hepaticas (which bloom at the same time) and the pink-and-gray fronds of the Japanese painted fern (*Athyrium niponicum* var. *pictum*). But now taxonomists say that Ross's mapleleaf must be called *Mukdenia rossii*, a forgettable name that may well doom it to horticultural obscurity.

Likewise with *Peltoboykinia watanabei*. Even I have to look for a label when visitors ask for the name of this plant. Again, the foliage looks as though it has been waxed, but the leaves are nearly circular and deeply cut into jagged lobes. In reasonably moist soil, each leaf measures 18" across and stands on a stalk at least as tall. The tiny yellow flowers, which appear on their own stalks in July, are nothing to swoon over, but they set copious seed that quickly turn a single plant into an effective groundcover in front of rhododendrons. Unwanted seedlings are easy to remove.

By contrast, everyone knows peonies, so why aren't the woodland species more popular in America? *Paeonia obovata* var. *alba* has flourished in the dappled shade of my woodland garden for 15 years. When this peony emerges in early spring, a coppery tone enhances the broadly lobed, graying leaves — a magnificent setting for large, white cups enhanced by golden stamens circling a crimson center. The flowers are fleeting, but the foliage remains quietly elegant during the summer months. As autumn turns the leaves to

When out of bloom, *Anemonopsis macrophylla* looks much like a bugbane, but a forest of branching 3' stems appears in August, carrying a profusion of lavender flowers shaped like small, nodding Japanese anemones. These are best seen dancing in a large drift, backed only by the deep green of a large-leaved rhododendron.

Anemonopsis macrophylla

burgundy, large seed capsules open to reveal a fuchsia lining, corrugated like crushed velvet and studded with blue "berries."

A decade ago I returned from an English vacation with a root of *Paeonia veitchii* var. *woodwardii*, which, to my delight, produces an entirely different garden effect. The stems of this fast-growing peony support deeply cut, light green leaves arranged in a mound of weeping layers 2' high and a yard across, decorated in May by drooping pink cups. Not a true woodland species, *P. veitchii* comes from Chinese "yak meadows," which I take to mean that, transported to sea level, the plant needs some direct sun but also shade during the hottest hours of the day. In my woods both peonies produce self-sown seedlings that reach blooming size in three to four years. If they are rare, it must be because they lack a good publicist.

So does *Glaucidium palmatum*, a fair substitute for the fabled and difficult Himalayan blue poppy (*Meconopsis betonicifolia*). Actually a member of the buttercup family, Japan's lavender "poppy" is the bold-leaved plant I depend upon to flourish even in dry soil and deep shade. As the name implies, the lobed leaves are shaped like a hand, 14" across, and two are borne atop each 26"-tall stem. The flowers are usually a soft lavender, although white and deep purple occasionally appear. In my garden, they open in late April, a perfect counterpoint to yellow primroses.

It's curious that the islands that gave us *Acer palmatum*, the Japanese maple, are so rich in herbaceous plants with foliage shaped like hands or maple leaves. *Kirengeshoma palmata* is another of these plants, and when I began making a garden in my woods it was a rarity. Today it is widely available and is often recommended for its September crop of clear yellow, twisted bell flowers. But the strong, arching 3'-tall stalks carrying 7" lobed leaves can also add an architectural element to the woodland garden. Rather late to appear in spring, this is an excellent plant to fill the airspace above summer-weary primroses and those wildflowers that go dormant by June.

Also widely available is *Polygonatum odoratum* var. *pluriflorum* 'Variegatum', an elegant Japanese Solomon's seal that has such short rhizomes that the plant appears as a clump. The 24"-tall stalks are nearly upright and are clothed top to bottom with broad leaves delicately banded in white — a charming contrast to plants with much-divided foliage, such as *Cimicifuga japonica*, a bugbane that makes 15"-high mounds of compound leaves. The 2' wands of pink buds and white flowers appear in September.

Sometimes there is no substitute for a really big plant of statuesque proportions. In a woodland garden, where the massive columns of tree trunks must be visually related to the delicate leaves of ferns and wildflowers, the intermediary agent is often a large rhododendron. Where space is tight in my garden a rodgersia does the same job. Named in honor of a U.S. navy admiral who headed an expedition to Japan before the turn of the century, these plants of enormous dignity can reach massive proportions in moist soil. (With my gravelly soil I must be content with a mere 4.5'.) The bronzed leaves of *Rodgersia aesculifolia* are especially elegant: a whorl of eight leaflets, each up to 10" long and deeply quilted by veins.

For a while, *Astilboides tabularis* was a rodgersia and now it's not. No matter what it's called, however, I think of this awesome yet somehow comical plant as a cluster of soda-fountain tables. Balanced on a 3' stem, each round leaf is nearly flat, gently scalloped, 3' in diameter and colored a kelly green that is as shiny as baked-on enamel. To achieve its full potential the plant needs to be kept pumped up with plenty of water. Like so many objects with fine and simple lines, *A. tabularis* is wonderful on its own — by a pool,

for example. But it can be put to more pedestrian uses, provided it has companions that can hold their own.

Lacking swampy land — but determined to grow this spectacular plant — I achieved an artificially high "water table" by burying a large tub, half filled with gravel before peaty soil was shoveled in, so the rim lies about 4" below the crown of the plant. Leo Blanchette, a local nurseryman who shares my enthusiasm for Asian woodland plants, says that a pinch of fertilizer once a month during the growing season helps encourage lushness. Is all this effort worthwhile? Hey, we're talking sculpture here, not just architecture!

To create a focal point at the end of a long grass path, I've planted these Chinese "tables" next to a *Hydrangea quercifolia* that flaunts large, oak-shaped leaves in the dappled shade of a katsura tree. In front there's a drift of *Hakonechloa macra* 'Aureola', one of Japan's finest plants for light shade. I first saw this magnificent golden grass arching over the edge of a large container on Harold Epstein's terrace. Years later, it is still listed by many authorities as being 1' tall, but in fact this slowly spreading grass can, when set free in acid, humus-rich soil, easily reach twice that height.

An American hydrangea, a Japanese grass and a Chinese vegetative table, all growing together in a wooded garden north of Boston: they're a reminder of ancient connections to a world that was once, quite literally, one. As for the pioneering gardener who taught so many of us about Asian foliage plants, I think I'll remember him by planting some clumps of *Epimedium epsteinii*. Tribute, after all, should be paid.

Kirengeshoma palmata

chapter three

DESIGNING WITH PERENNIALS

PERENNIALS WITH GOLD FOLIAGE

wisely placed gold adds welcome sparkle

by GLENN WITHEY

Whether to brighten a dark corner, to relieve the tedium of an otherwise monochromatic border, or to create a color-themed garden, golden-leaved perennials are invaluable.

They are also remarkably versatile. Plants with yellow foliage can be used as a contrast (for example, with blue-leaved plants), act as a bridge with cream- and white-variegated plants, or serve as a mediator between hot and cool colors. The great strength of yellow is its ability to harmonize with all other colors (the one exception being a brassy gold with a cool pink), though it is important to remember that yellow carries the farthest, visually speaking, of any color.

To cite an extreme example, a plant as potentially large as *Robinia pseudoacacia* 'Frisia' demands careful thought when you are deciding where to place it, otherwise it will dominate the entire garden. Though the scale of most golden-leaved perennials is much smaller, they still require careful placement so that they will complement rather than overwhelm their neighbors. But resist the temptation to dot yellow-foliaged plants all over the garden.

Instead, concentrate on specific areas: the repetition of one or two kinds of plants, or of a certain shape, is usually much more effective.

The different groups of golden-leaved plants lend themselves to different seasonal strategies. Whereas golden conifers and broadleaved evergreens can add winter sparkle to a garden, the majority of the yellow-leaved perennials are spring-into-summer beauties.

Bear in mind that certain gold-leaved plants are likely to burn or turn coppery if exposed to too much sun. (Full sun in the Pacific Northwest, however, is not the same as full sun in South Carolina.) Others may turn chartreuse if planted in shade that is too deep. You may need to move a plant several times before finding the spot that is just right.

Depending on your point of view, the spring-blooming *Dicentra spectabilis* 'Gold Heart' (USDA Zones 3–9; 2'–3') is either heaven or fingernails on a blackboard. The bright foliage emerges early and the warm rose-pink flowers add zing. If the plant is well fed and watered you can cut the foliage down to the ground after flowering and expect regrowth.

Above left: Emerging from a tight tuft in the spring, *Veronica prostrata* 'Trehane' (Zones 4–9; 3"–8") is a delightful small spreader that never becomes unruly. If sheared back hard after flowering and treated well with extra helpings of water and fertilizer, 'Trehane' will respond with fresh new foliage for the rest of the season. **Lower left** *Carex elata* 'Aurea' (Zones 5–9; to 2.5') needs careful siting. Moist soil in part shade is absolutely essential for success. The narrow leaves provide good contrast with blue-leaved hostas, *Astilboides tabularis,* and other bold brethren. **Above right:** The spiky-looking yet friendly *Yucca filamentosa* 'Color Guard' (Zones 5–10; 4'–6') is at its best in winter when the plant glows with subtle, rosy-pink flushes to the edges of the leaves. Underplant it with black mondo grass (*Ophiopogon planiscapus* 'Nigrescens') for an intense contrast. **Lower right:** *Hosta* 'Sum and Substance' (Zones 3–9) is a real workhorse. Sun-tolerant in most parts of the country, this monster can reach 6' across and 3' tall if well-fed. The bold leaves provide an excellent foil for grassy or filigreed foliage.

Above left: The vibrant spears (to 18") of *Iris pallida* 'Variegata' (Zones 4–9) emerge in spring and then fade as summer progresses. This iris — which also bears pleasant, short-lived, blue-mauve flowers in late May — is best sited where it will not be overfed or overwatered. Small blue-leaved sedums and minor bulbs make good companions. **Lower left:** The fresh, vibrant, emerging foliage of *Filipendula ulmaria* 'Aurea' (Zones 3–9; 3'–6') — a springtime beauty that may fade or burn in summer — is one of the early welcomers to the new gardening season. Use later-emerging perennials as companions to carry the show in late summer. **Above right:** The color of the elegant, flowing woodland grass *Hakonechloa macra* 'Aureola' (Zones 5–9; to 14") is more pronounced in partial shade, while all-day sun can bleach the variegation. Usually, more than one plant should be used to create a flowing river or wave effect. **Lower right:** The best variegated comfrey on the market to date, *Symphytum ×uplandicum* 'Axminster Gold' (Zones 4–9; 2'–4') has stronger yellow, burn-resistant variegation that lasts through the season. If the plant becomes tatty after flowering, cut it to the ground for a flush of new foliage. *Cimicifuga simplex* 'Hillside Black Beauty' makes a good companion.

Above left: The intense spring coloration of *Lysimachia nummularia* 'Aurea' (Zones 3–8; 4"–8") is a welcome sight on cloudy days. This mat-forming groundcover provides a good foil for larger, dark-flowered, spring-blooming bulbs, such as the hyacinths 'Distinction' and 'Blue Magic'. Give it moist soil with partial shade, as it may burn in full sun. **Lower left:** *Tradescantia* 'Blue and Gold' (Zones 5–9; 2'–3') is a beautiful but somewhat un-gainly plant for partial shade. If it is fed too well, expect it to do a belly flop into the dirt. Interplanting it with sturdier, lower-growing neighbors such as *Hosta* 'Halcyon' or *Epimedium perralderianum* can help alleviate the problem. **Above right** *Stachys byzantina* 'Primrose Heron' (Zones 4–9; to 12") forms low, spreading mats of soft chartreuse, velvety leaves, which make a foil for some of the hardy geraniums that send out long, flowering arms, such as *G. ×riversleaianum* 'Russell Prichard'. Grooming throughout the summer is required; even then, it may mildew. **Lower right:** In the lower range of its hardiness zone, *Acanthus mollis* 'Hollard's Gold' (Zones 7–10; 3'–5') is slow to establish. Full sun can produce brassy, burnished leaves, while partial shade gives a chartreuse effect. It is highly useful for knitting together smaller perennials with golden-leaved trees or shrubs.

COLLECTING SILVER

this group of foliage plants adds a bright shine to any border

by Daniel J. Hinkley

Buddleia 'Lochinch'

The reason gardeners find silver-leaved plants so effective is the neutral zone they provide between conflicting colors.

At least this is what I've picked up from countless tomes on color theory and, tending to believe all I've read, I've perpetuated this view by repeating it to others. Silver, so the story goes, plays well within nearly any color: it is cool and elegant with deep blues, rich and spicy with reds and oranges, crisp and bracing with yellows and butterscotch — all while providing an effortless transition between opposing hues. I'm not arguing with these assertions — it's simply that I don't know if the supposition is based on scientific inquiry or simply personal preference.

Nonetheless, the reflective quality of silver-leaved plants does indeed make our gardens more inviting in the ebbing light of summer evenings — the only time of day that an increasing number of gardeners can find a moment to luxuriate in their landscapes. A vein of silver or pewter running through a border does indeed add a seal of refinement to any garden, providing a dose of Mediterranean radiance on a sunny summer day while conjuring up pure enchantment on moonlit nights.

That these plants evoke a climate of warmth and drought is not surprising, since their coloration is an adaptation that evolved to conserve moisture in the plants' tissues. Inspected under a microscope, this sheen is, in most plants, produced by overlapping, translucent scales or fine hairs that protect the plant tissue by reflecting desiccating light — all to our ultimate pleasure.

Surprisingly, a number of exceptionally hardy willows — a genus of plants known for their affinity for wet sites — possess superlative pewtered foliage. *Salix exigua* and *S. alba* var. *sericea* are large-growing trees to 45' or even more, but can easily be coppiced yearly to 3' to fit into smaller gardens. Both will accept a wide range of soil types, from overly wet to

Santolina pinnata 'Edward Bowles'

Salix exigua

average, well-drained loam. The elegantly long and narrow leaves of both shimmer with a platinum patina in a light summer breeze while offering a texture that is, well, willowy.

Much more demure — and equally easy-going — are three shrubby willows that don't require the yearly hack to the ground. *Salix helvetica* grows to 3' with an equal spread, and bears narrow, somewhat leathery leaves of grayish silver. In a sunny part of our Seattle-area garden (USDA Zone 8), the sturdy, upright stems both physically and visually support the nonvining *Clematis integrifolia*. In midsummer, this clematis is capped with deep blue flowers that look extraordinary nestled amid the willow's mirrored foliage. *Salix lanata* is somewhat larger — to 4' × 4', with oval leaves of woolly silver — while *S. repens* var. *argentea* sports small, rounded leaves of silver gray along trailing stems to 5'. These willows, all of which are hardy from Zones 2 to 10, produce the typical crop of catkins in earliest spring, offering the bonus of branches for forcing throughout winter. Of course, one may also simply enjoy the catkins' effect before the foliage emerges.

The weeping silver-leaved pear, *Pyrus salicifolia* 'Pendula' (Zones 4–8), possesses olivelike leaves of silvery green borne along weeping branches from an upright trunk to 20'. Though a well-grown specimen looks like grace incarnate, those who have struggled with training this tree know that it displays all the restraint of a Labrador pup. From time to time, formerly pendulous branches suddenly decide to rise skyward and must be removed religiously. But even unruly puppy dogs are loveable, and if well trained, grow up to be outstanding companions. It's the same with the silver-leaved pear. We grow *Clematis montana* var. *rubens* 'Freda' through its branches, thus creating for several weeks in late spring the spectacle of rich pink flowers nestled among the gray foil of the pear's foliage — an endearing companionship admired by all except perhaps the pear.

E. umbellata, the autumn olive, and *Elaeagnus angustifolia*, the Russian olive, have been grown for years as windbreaks and wildlife cover, but ultimately at considerable costs to our native ecosystems across the upper-tier states. Tolerant of a wide range of soil types and bearing fruit attractive to birds, these two species have spread well beyond their intended areas of use. There are other selections of *Elaeagnus*, however, that have proven much more restrained in their procreational activities. The British hybrid *E.* 'Quicksilver' (Zones 4–9) perhaps possesses the most dramatic silver foliage of any hardy plant that I grow. 'Quicksilver' is a deciduous shrub to 15' or slightly more, with shimmering platinum leaves up to 3" long. Extremely hardy and drought tolerant, its most endearing trait is its sterility, which ensures that no errant seedlings will appear outside the garden.

Though needing a protected site in colder parts of North America, the evergreen *E. pungens* (Zones 6–10) offers its reflective leaves of gray-green throughout the year. Forming a rounded shrub to 6' × 6', it offers a bonus of mid-autumn flowers that pack a powerful punch of fragrance yet seldom result in fruit under cultivation. Though I have seen this species successfully grown as an espaliered wall shrub in a Zone 6 Delaware garden, it performs better for gardeners in Zone 7 and above. It is deserving of much wider use in these milder areas of this country.

The butterfly bushes, of the genus *Buddleia*, are mostly thought of as vigorous shrubs that produce deliciously fragrant flowers in late summer. Though we use a number of them in our mixed borders for their floral effect, their summer and winter foliage is much less ephemeral. Though most buddleias are technically deciduous, if given a sharp pruning directly after flowering, the resulting new growth will retain its foliage throughout winter. More than once we have had winter visitors mistake these shrubs for eucalyptus — a testament to their foliar effectiveness. One of the most outstanding in this regard is *Buddleia* 'Lochinch', with soft lavender panicles of flowers in mid-July amid lovely silvery gray foliage. Better yet is *B. nivea*, with cottony leaves and stems of brilliant white felt (its floral attributes are of little merit).

Santolina pinnata is a low-growing, evergreen, drought-tolerant shrub or subshrub to 30" that lends itself well to formal hedging, as it tolerates a substantial amount of shearing. In summer, brassy yellow

Pyrus salicifolia 'Pendula'

Astelia chathamica 'Silver Spear'

buttons appear on willowy stems above filigreed, intensely silver foliage. I confess I dislike these two colors in tandem, and so I find the selection 'Edward Bowles', with soft, pastel yellow flowers, much more palatable. *Santolina pinnata* is hardy from Zones 7 to 10, and requires full sun and well-drained soil. In colder climates, consider using laciniated-leaved cultivars of dusty miller (*Senecio cineraria*), which has equally dazzling foliage.

Ozothamnus rosmarinifolius, a shrub that hails from Australia, is surprisingly hardy, surviving temperatures as low as 5°F (Zone 7). Requiring full sun and baked, well-drained soil, it provides superb texture with its needlelike foliage in metallic tones of silver and gray. In summer, clusters of pretty white flowers open from rich pink buds. Ultimately maturing to 6' or more, it can be cut back hard on a regular basis to rejuvenate its form and foliage. We have found this shrub to be perfectly suited to containers, where it contrasts dramatically with the bold blades of a purple phormium.

Sadly tender in our climate are two genera from New Zealand that are the envy of keen gardeners around the globe. Fortunately, like *O. rosmarinifolius*, many of the species can be grown in containers. *Astelia chathamica* 'Silver Spear' (hardy in Zones 9–11) produces delectable, upright swords of shimmering platinum that add a remarkable presence to any container planting. In the open ground it requires full sun and well-drained soil. Several species of *Celmisia* are perhaps even more remarkable, though their reputation for being difficult is somewhat justified by their need for exceptionally well drained soil. With that said, we successfully grow *C. alpina* in containers, where it produces compact clumps of jagged, upright, shimmering foliage to 10".

In the end, I am uncertain exactly why I have become so smitten by silver-leaved plants, but in gardening, strenuous rationalization is seldom called for if it feels right. Like many before me, as I have grown more self-assured in my garden, I have jettisoned the color wheel. I now include silver plants for the same reason I include all the other plants in my garden — I simply like them.

Salix lanata

suppliers

Perennials

AVANT GARDENS
710 High Hill Road
North Dartmouth, MA 02747
www.avantgardensne.com
Online catalog

BLUESTONE PERENNIALS
7211 Middle Ridge Rd.
Madison, OH 44057-3096
www.bluestoneperennials.com
Free catalog

BURPEE
300 Park Avenue
Warminster, PA 18974
www.burpee.com
Free catalog

CANYON CREEK NURSERY
3527 Dry Creek Road
Oroville, CA 95965
www.canyoncreeknursery.com
Online catalog

DIGGING DOG
P.O. Box 471
Albion, CA 95410
www.diggingdog.com
Online catalog

FIELDSTONE GARDENS
55 Quaker Lane
Vassalboro, ME 04989-3816
www.fieldstonegardens.com
Catalog $2.50

FORESTFARM
990 Tetherow Road
Williams, OR 97544-9599
www.forestfarm.com
Free catalog

HERONSWOOD NURSERY
7530 Northeast 288th Street
Kingston, WA 98346
www.heronswood.com
Catalog $5

HIGH COUNTRY GARDENS
2902 Rufina Street
Santa Fe, NM 87505
www.highcountrygardens.com
Free catalog

KLEHM'S SONG SPARROW PERENNIAL FARM
13101 East Rye Road
Avalon, WI 53505
www.klehm.com
Free catalog

MONROVIA NURSERIES
Available through retail outlets
www.monrovia.com
Online catalog

OAKES DAYLILIES
P.O. Box 268
Corryton, TN 37721
www.oakesdaylilies.com
Online catalog

PLANT DELIGHTS NURSERY
9241 Sauls Road
Raleigh, NC 27603
www.plantdelights.com
Free catalog

PRAIRIE NURSERY
P.O. Box 306
Westfield, WI 53964
www.prairienursery.com
Online catalog

PROVEN WINNERS
550 West State Street
Suite D
Sycamore, IL 60178
Available through retail outlets
www.provenwinners.com

SENECA HILL PERENNIALS
3712 County Route 57
Oswego, NY 13126
www.senecahill.com
Free catalog

SCHREINER'S IRIS GARDENS
3625 Quinaby Road N.E.
Salem, OR 97303
www.schreinersgardens.com
Free catalog

SINGING SPRINGS NURSERY
8802 Wilkerson Road
Cedar Grove, NC 27231
www.singingspringsnursery.com
Free catalog

VAN BOURGONDIEN
P.O. Box 1000
Babylon, NY 11702
www.vanbourgondien.com
Free catalog

ANDRÉ VIETTE FARM & NURSERY
P.O. Box 1109
Fishersville, VA 22939
www.inthegardenradio.com
Online catalog

WAYSIDE GARDENS
1 Garden Lane
Hodges, SC 29695
www.waysidegardens.com
Free catalog

WHITE FLOWER FARM

P.O. Box 50, Route 63

Litchfield, CT 06759

www.whiteflowerfarm.com

Free catalog

GILBERT H. WILD & SON

3044 State Highway 37

Sarcoxie, MO 64862-0338

www.gilberthwild.com

Catalog $3

Ornamental grasses

EARTHLY PURSUITS

2901 Kuntz Road

Windsor Mill, MD 21244

www.earthlypursuits.net

Online catalog

LIMEROCK ORNAMENTAL GRASSES

70 Sawmill Road

Port Matilda, PA 16870

www.limerockgrasses.com

Online catalog

Seeds

THE COOK'S GARDEN

P.O. Box 1889

Southampton, PA 18966-0895

Free catalog

FRAGRANT GARDEN NURSERY

P.O. Box 4246

Brookings, OR 97415

www.fragrantgarden.com

Online catalog

FRANKLIN HILL SEEDS

2430 Rochester Road

Sewickly, PA 15143-8667

www.franklinhillseeds.com

Free catalog

HARRIS SEEDS

355 Paul Road

P.O. Box 22960

Rochester, NY 14624-0966

www.harrisseeds.com

Free catalog

J.L. HUDSON, SEEDSMAN

Star Route 2, Box 337

La Honda, CA 94020

www.jlhudsonseeds.net

Free catalog

JOHNNY'S SELECTED SEEDS

955 Benton Avenue

Winslow, ME 04901

www.johnnyseeds.com

Free catalog

MIKAMOKI SEEDS

66 South Orchard Street

Logan, OH 43138

www.mikamoki.com

Online catalog

PARK SEED

1 Parkton Avenue

Greenwood, SC 29647

www.parkseed.com

Free catalog

PINETREE GARDEN SEEDS

P.O. Box 300

New Gloucester, ME 04260

www.superseeds.com

Free catalog

RENEE'S GARDEN SEEDS

7389 W. Zayante Rd.

Felton, CA 95018

www.reneesgarden.com

Online catalog

SELECT SEEDS

180 Stickney Hill Road

Union, CT 06076

www.selectseeds.com

Online catalog

SHEFFIELD'S SEED COMPANY

269 Auburn Road, Route 34

Locke, New York 13092

www.sheffields.com

Online catalog

STOKES SEEDS

P.O. Box 548

Buffalo, NY 14240-0548

www.stokeseeds.com

Free catalog

THOMPSON & MORGAN SEEDSMEN

P.O. Box 1308

Jackson, NJ 08527-0308

www.thompson-morgan.com

Online catalog

VESEY'S SEEDS

P.O. Box 9000

Charlottetown, PE

Canada, C1A 8K6

www.veseys.com

Free catalog

WILDSEED FARMS

425 Wildflower Hills

Fredericksburg, TX. 78624

www.wildseedfarms.com

Free catalog

index